CUTTING PRACTICE FOR PRESCHOOLERS

A Fun Step 1 Scissor Skills Activity Workbook
With Coloring Sheets, Animals, Shapes, Patterns,
Beginner Cut and Paste
for Toddlers and Kids Ages 3–5

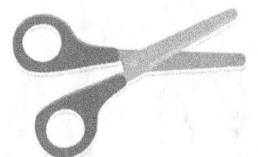

Scholastic Panda
Education

ISBN: 978-1-953149-44-2

THIS BOOK BELONGS TO:

Free Coloring Book for Kids!

This fun printable coloring book is a blast and keeps

kids engaged for hours!

It's filled with cute doodles, animals, and so much more!

Get Your Copy Here:

https://bit.ly/3dfULwO

SCISSOR SKILLS INSTRUCTIONS

We are so excited your child is building upon some critical skills that will serve them for the rest of their life!

Did you know that opening and closing scissors using the muscles in your hand, you are practicing fine motor skills?

In fact, fine motor skills are also essential for when children begin learning to write.

Scissors skills also play a crucial role in helping children develop hand-eye coordination – Holding the paper in one hand and the scissors in the other, they will practice guiding the scissors as they move across the paper.

Let's review a few important points before using this book

Learning scissor skills can be a challenge for all involved, especially for those teaching!

Follow these simple, effective tips to set yourself up for success:

SCISSOR SAFTEY – Make it clear that scissors are only for cutting paper and nothing else! Safety is the top priority, so no walking with scissors.

QUALITY – Get a good pair of scissors, ideally with a blunt point, yet sharp enough to cut paper.

POSITIONING – Help your child hold the scissors correctly. If your child is left-handed, be sure to purchase left-handed scissors.

ENCOURAGEMENT – Start slow and remember ... progress is always made through practice!

STRAIGHT LINES

Practice cutting straight lines as you cut the dotted line along each string.

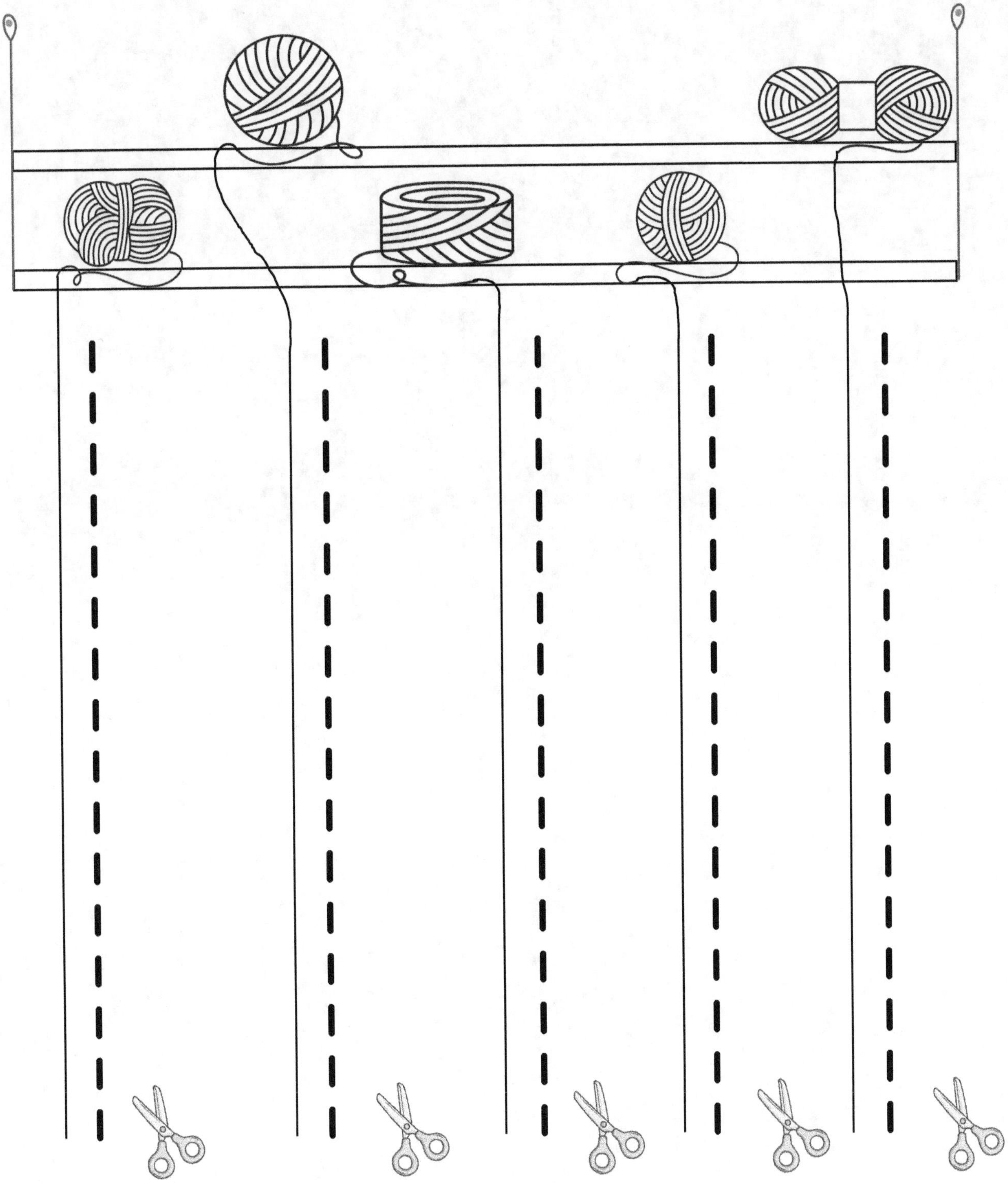

STRAIGHT LINES

LEVEL

Cut the straight dashed lines to help each animal get to the other side of the page!

CURVY LINES & BALLOONS

Carefully cut each curvy balloon string. Don't forget to color each balloon!

CURVY LINES & KITES

Color each kite then cut each string before they fly way!

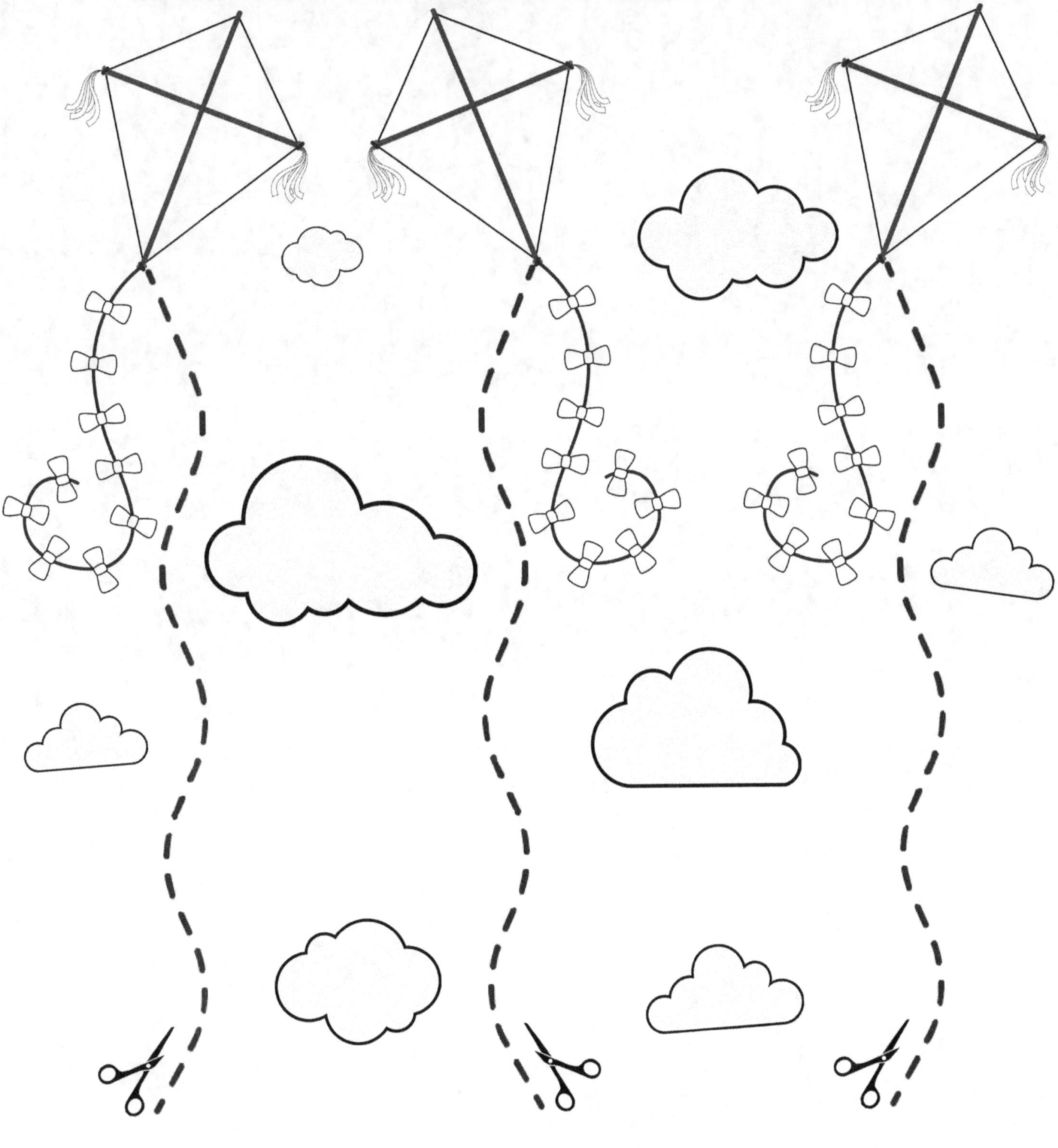

ZIGZAGS & SEAHORSES

Color the sea life then practice cutting zigzags

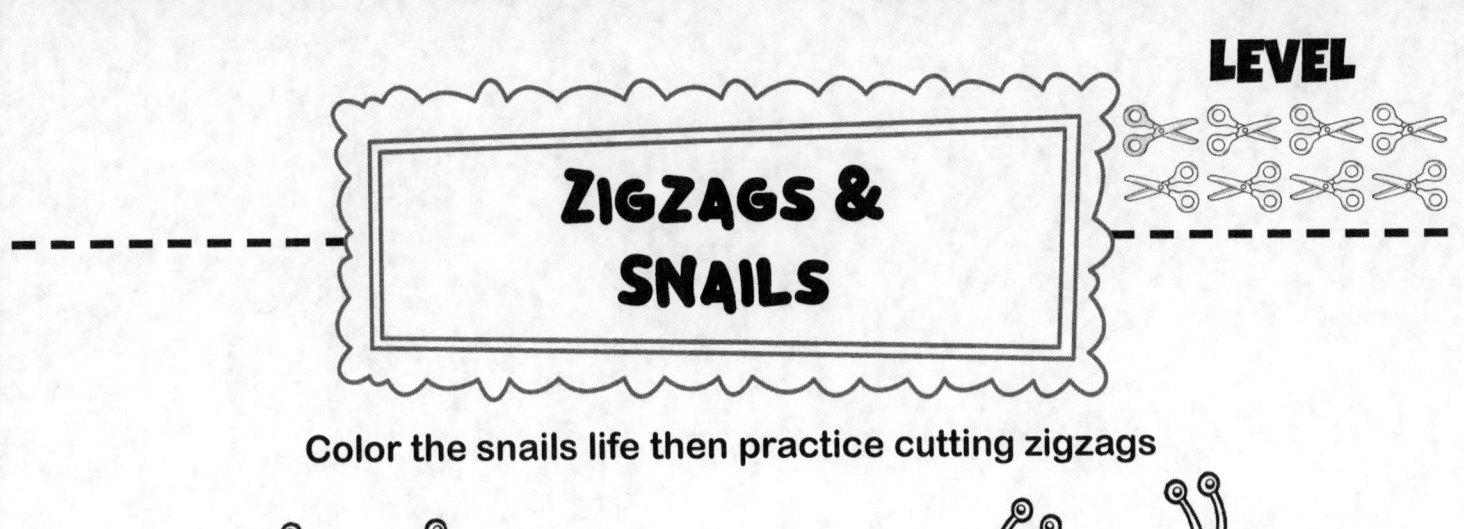

ZIGZAGS & SNAILS

Color the snails life then practice cutting zigzags

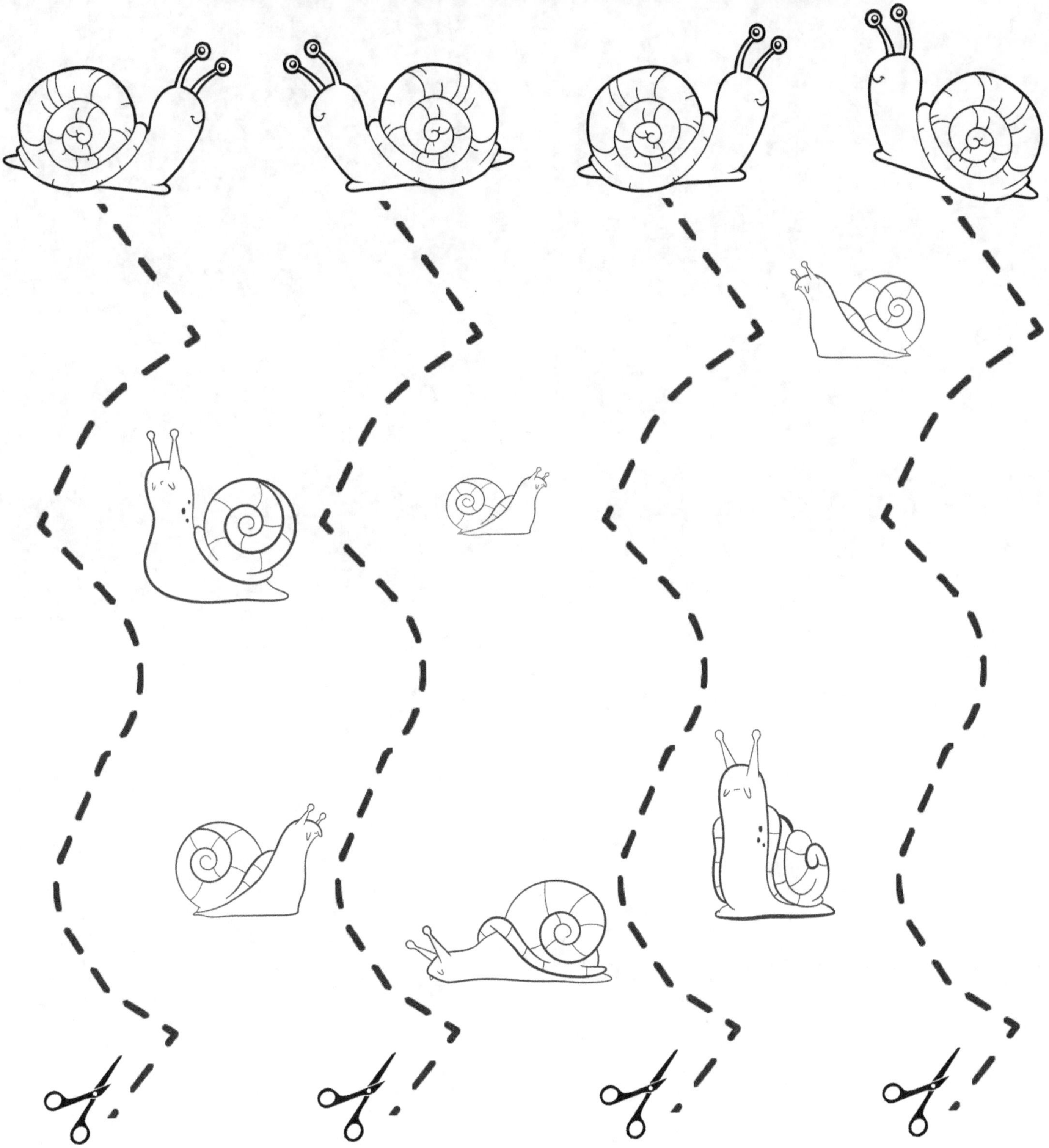

SPIRAL & SNOWFLAKES

Let's practice cutting a spiral! Don't forget to color the snowflakes.

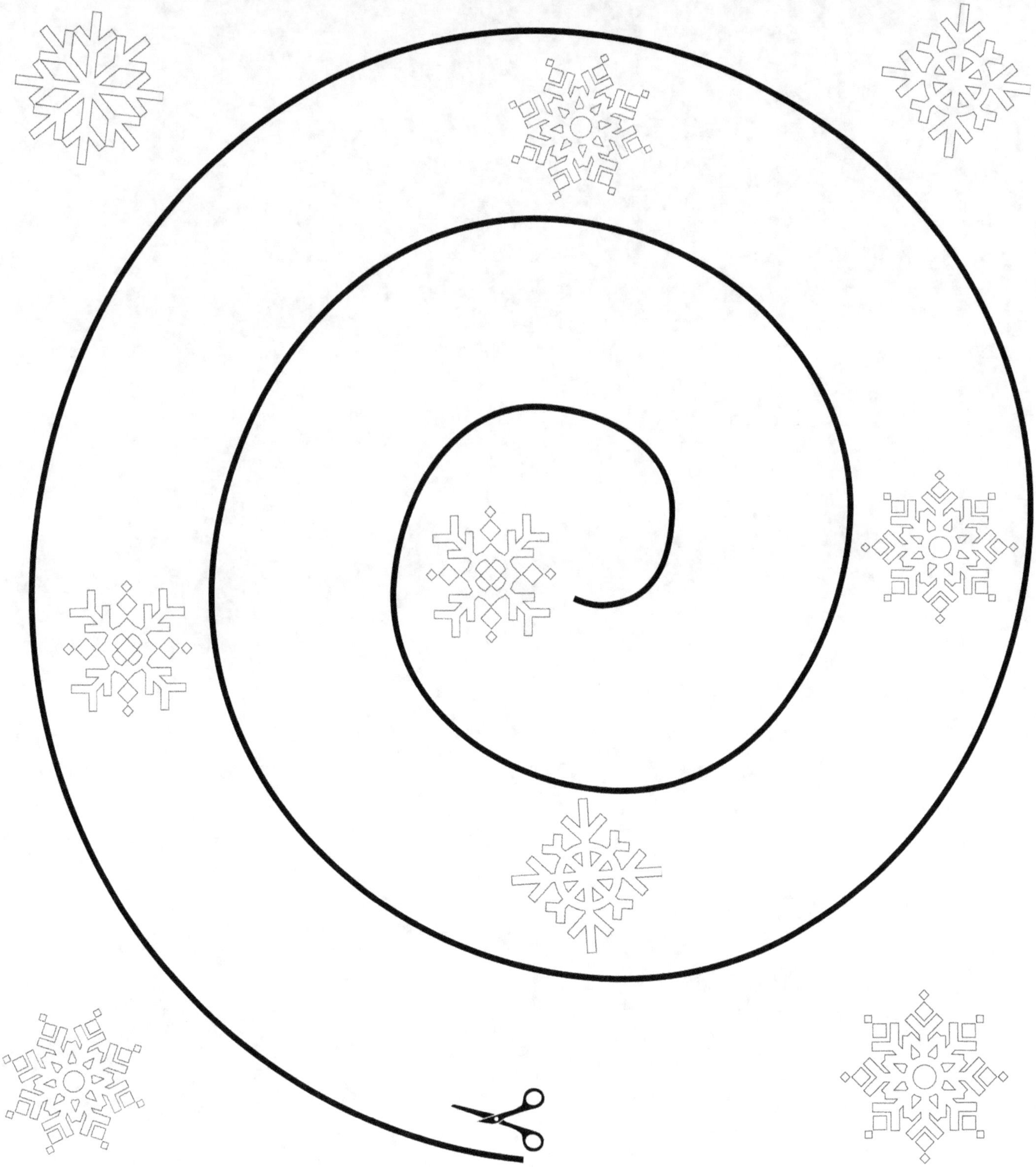

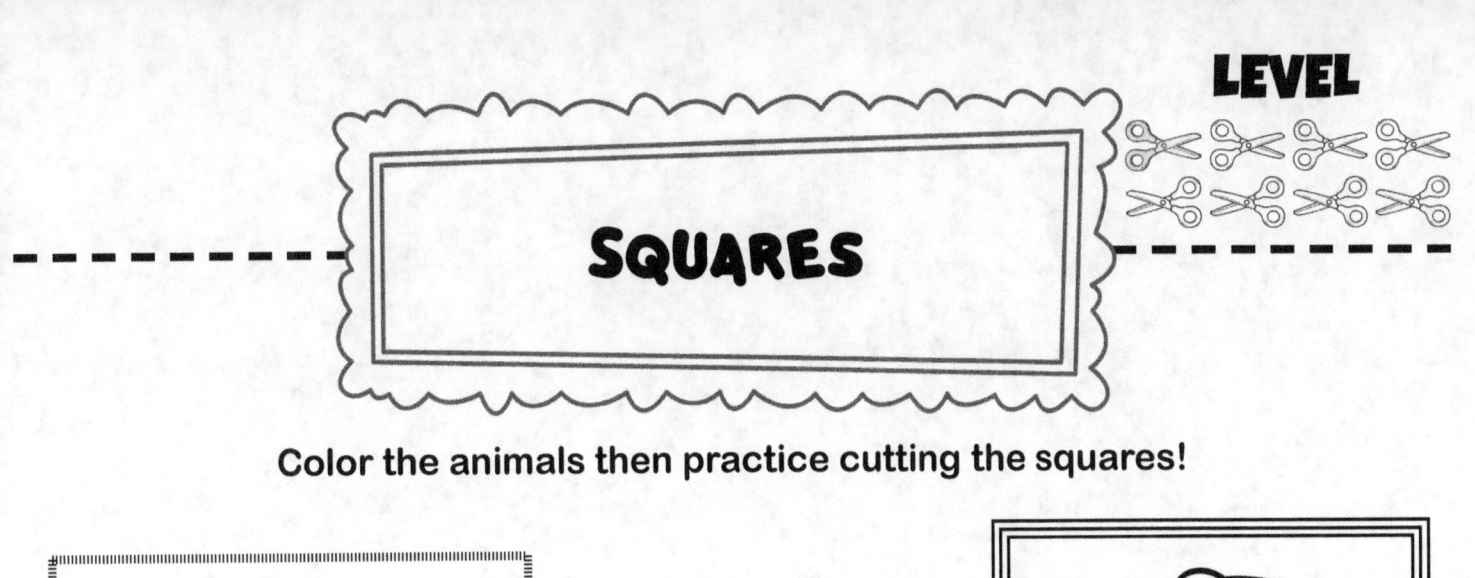

SQUARES

Color the animals then practice cutting the squares!

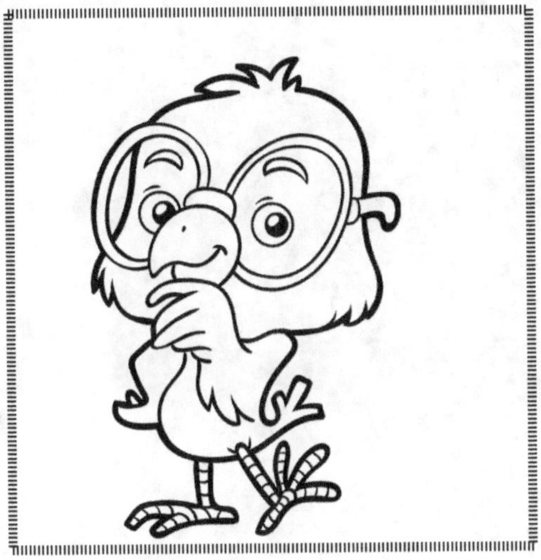

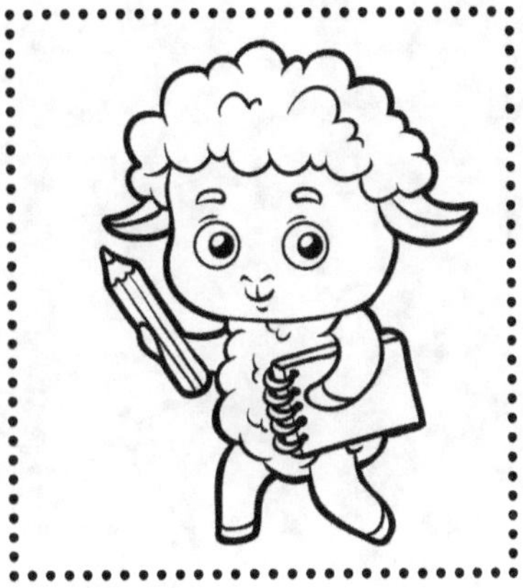

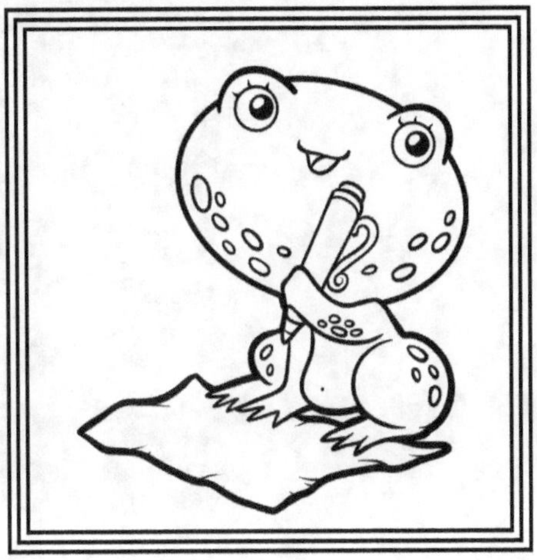

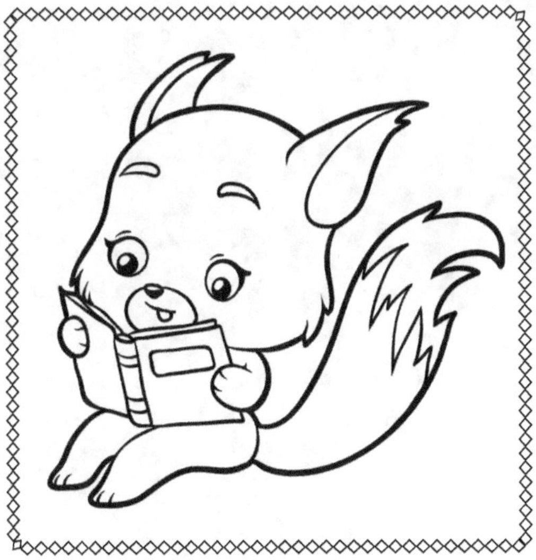

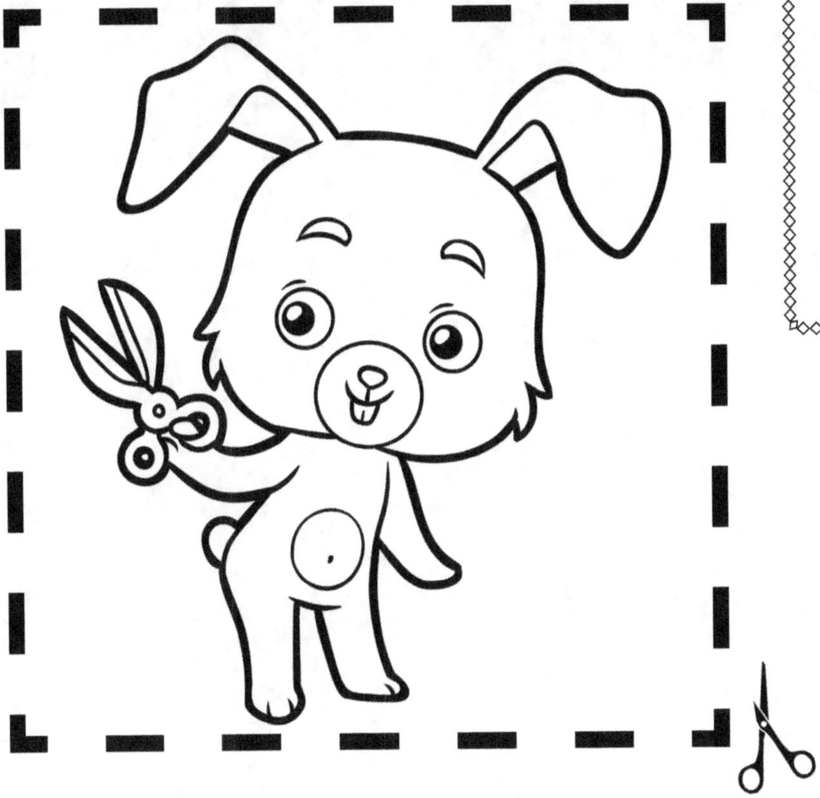

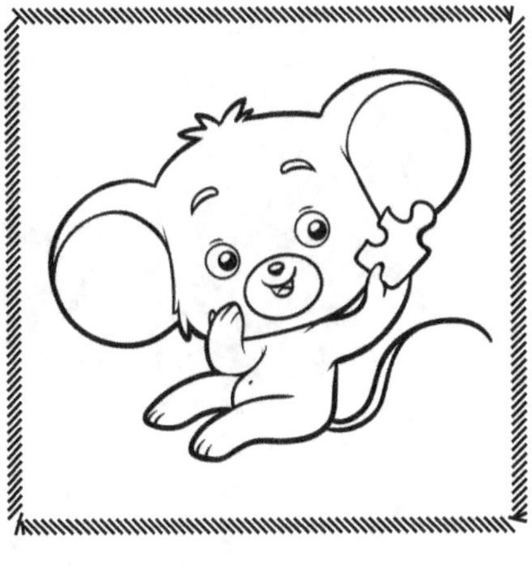

CIRCLES

Color the cats and then let's practice cutting some circles!

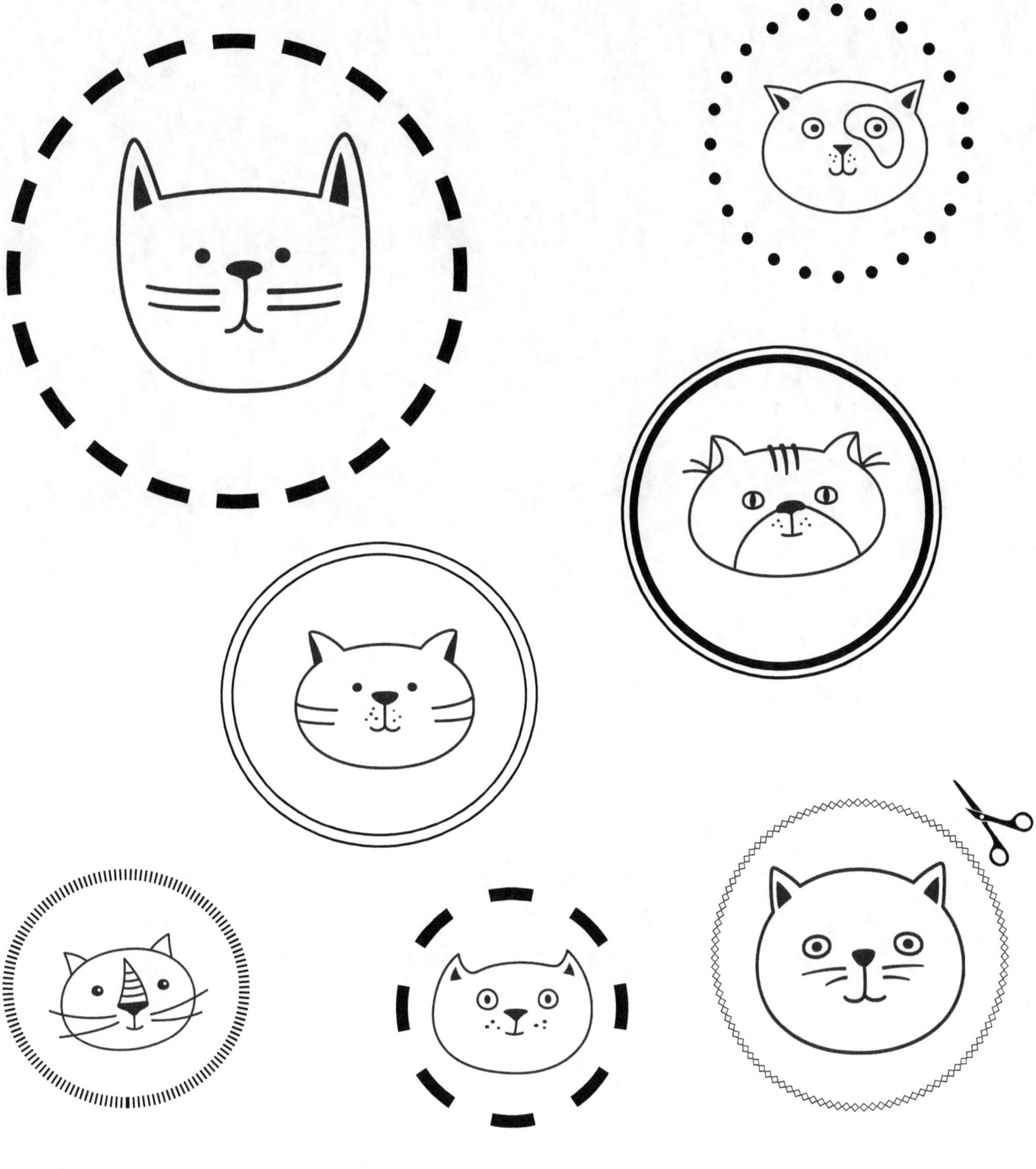

HEARTS

Take your time practicing slowly cutting out each heart!

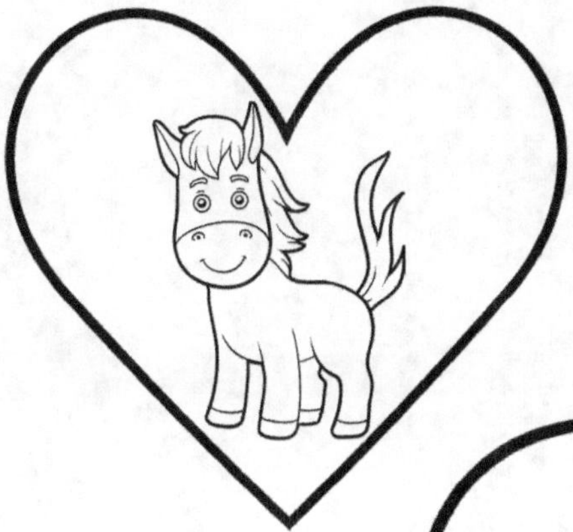

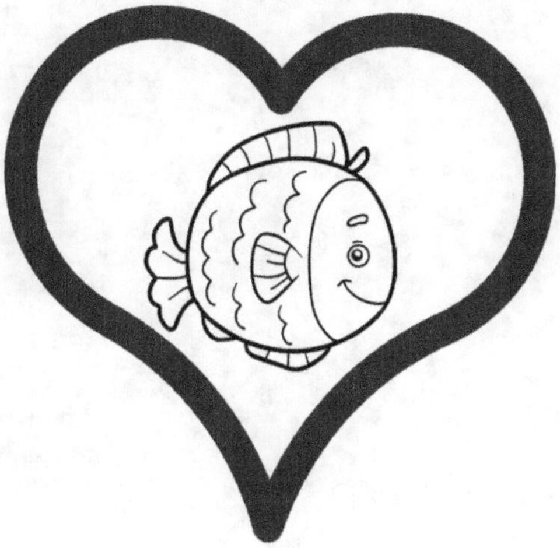

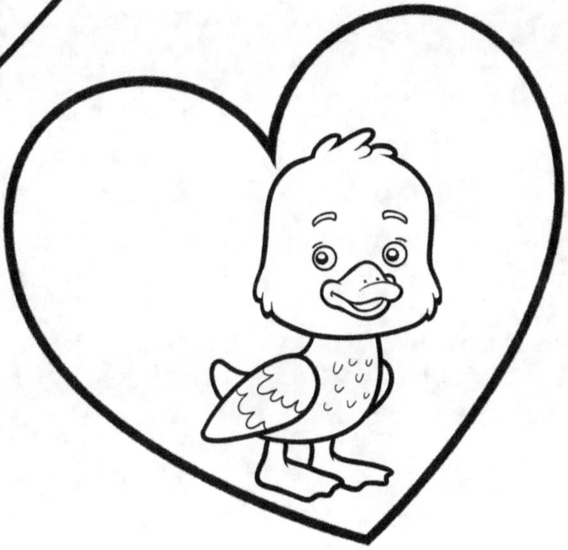

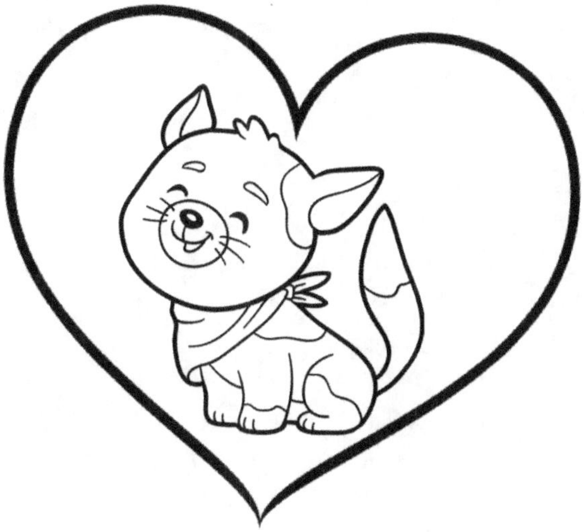

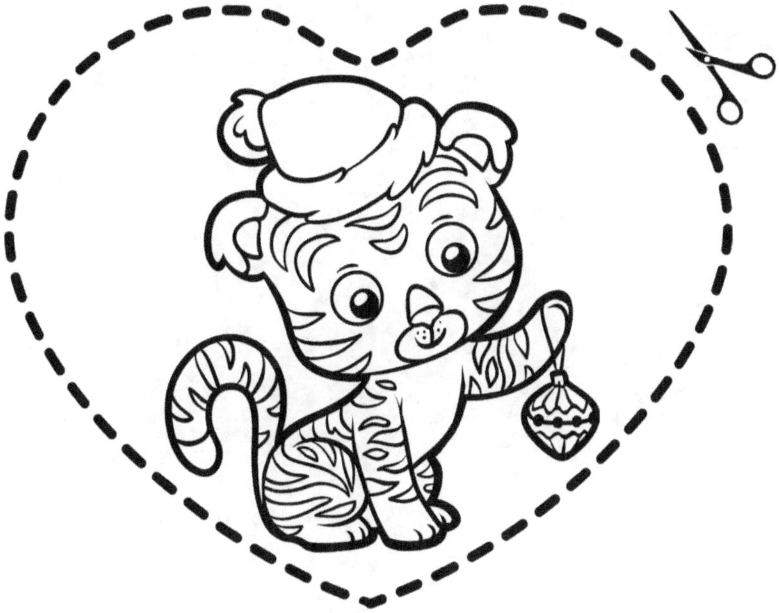

TRIANGLES

Color and cut out the triangles

LEVEL

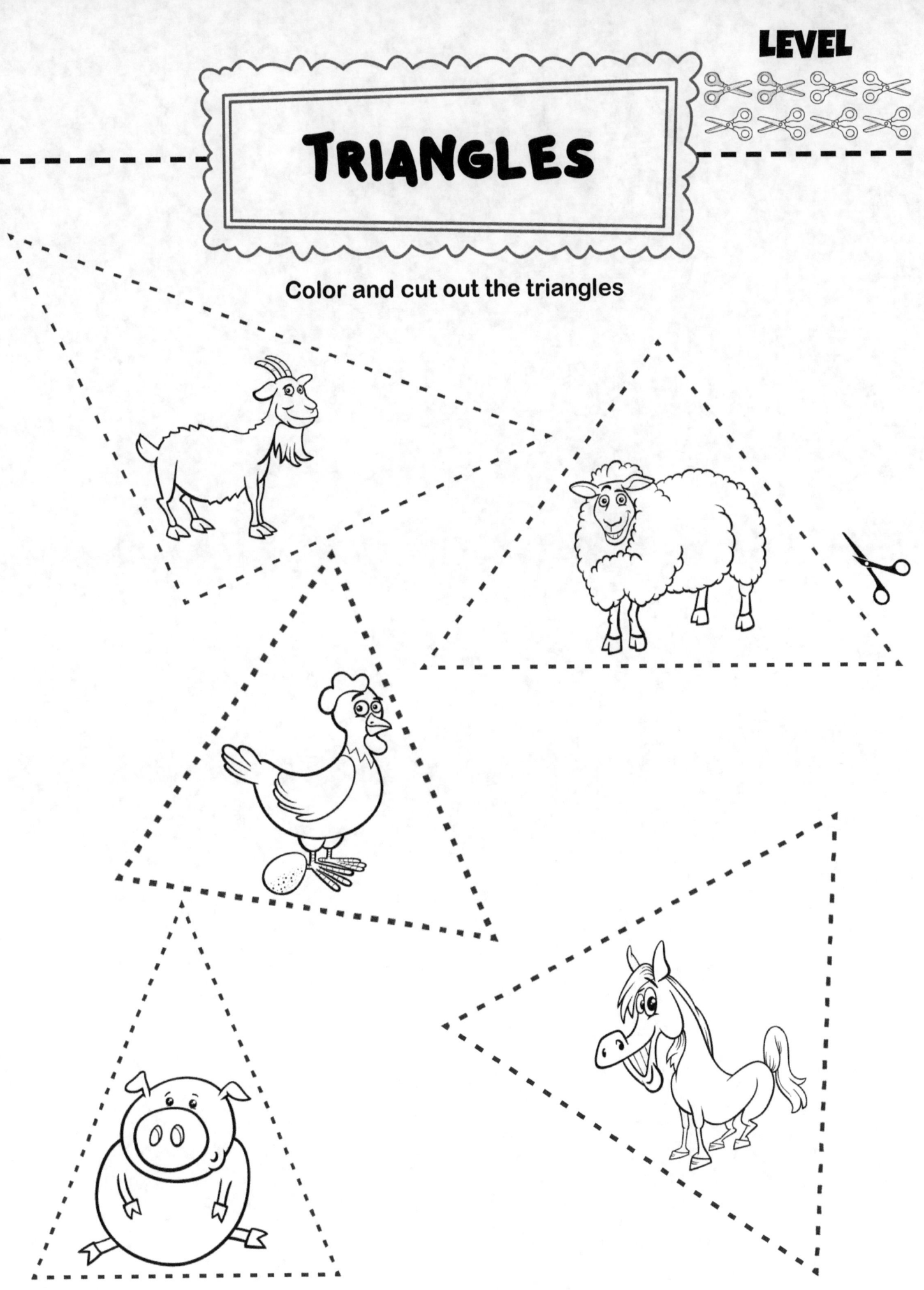

CHOCOLATE BAR

Color and cut out the chocolate bar

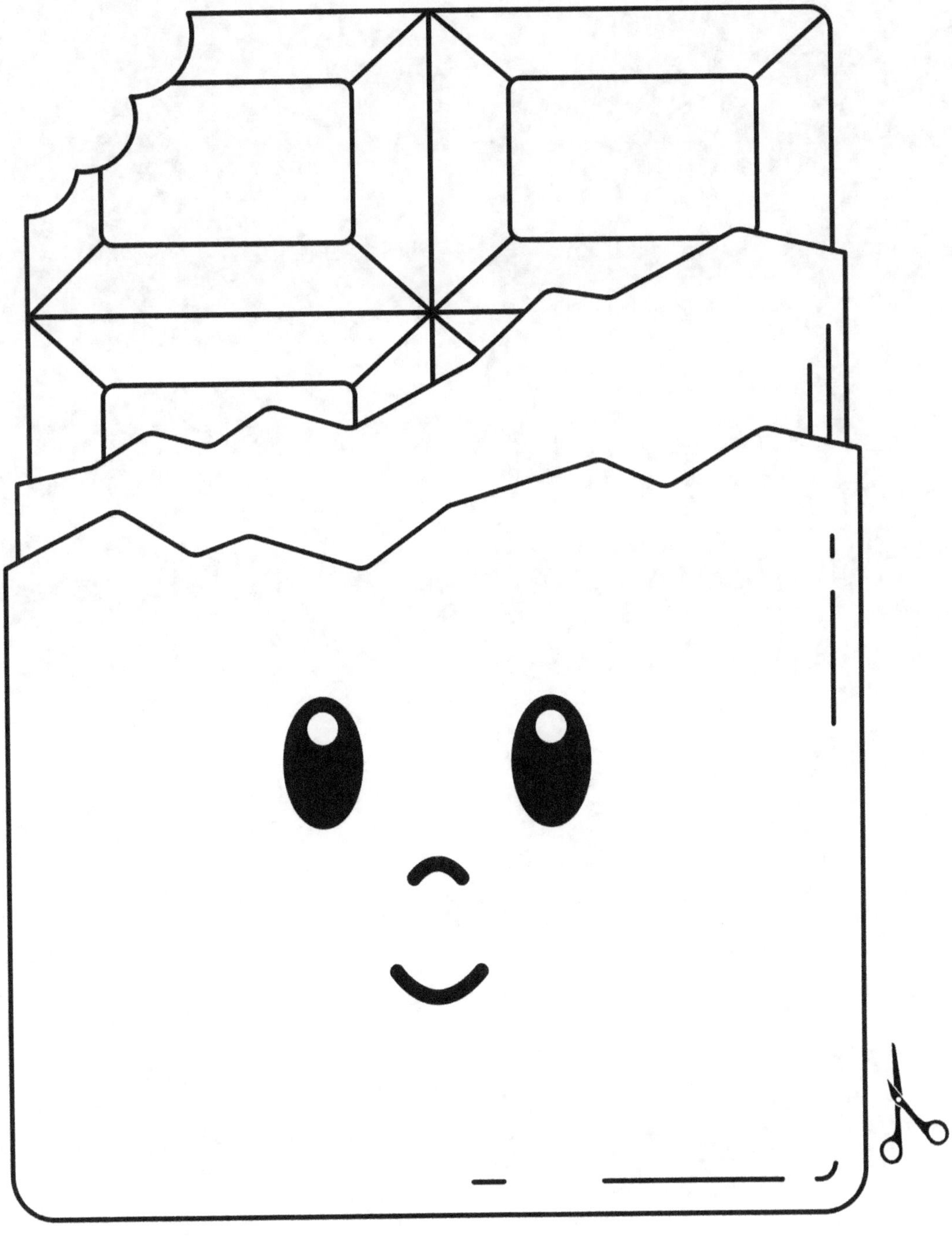

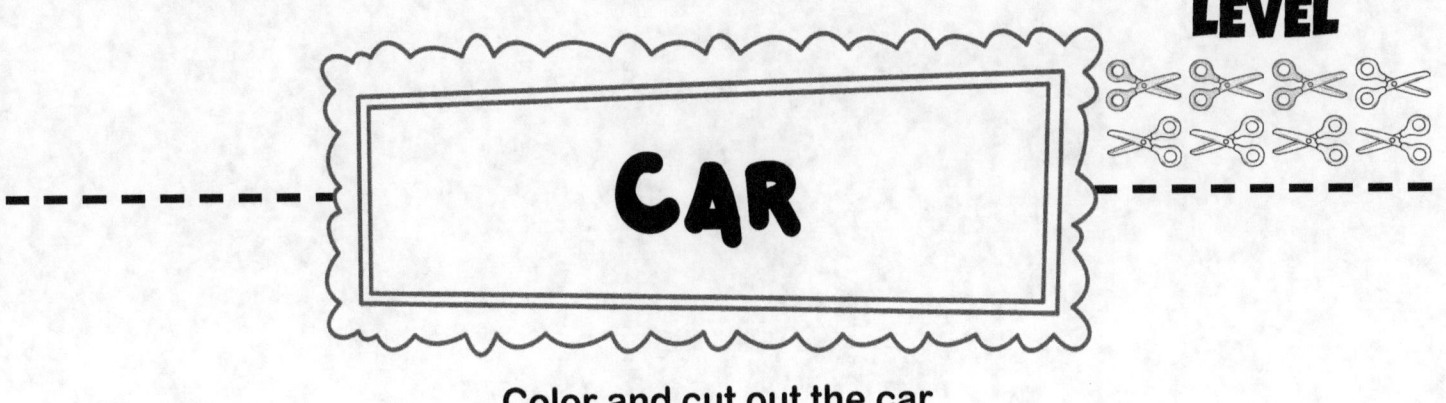

CAR

LEVEL

Color and cut out the car

STARFISH

LEVEL

Color and cut out the starfish

WIZARD HAT

Color and cut out the wizard hat

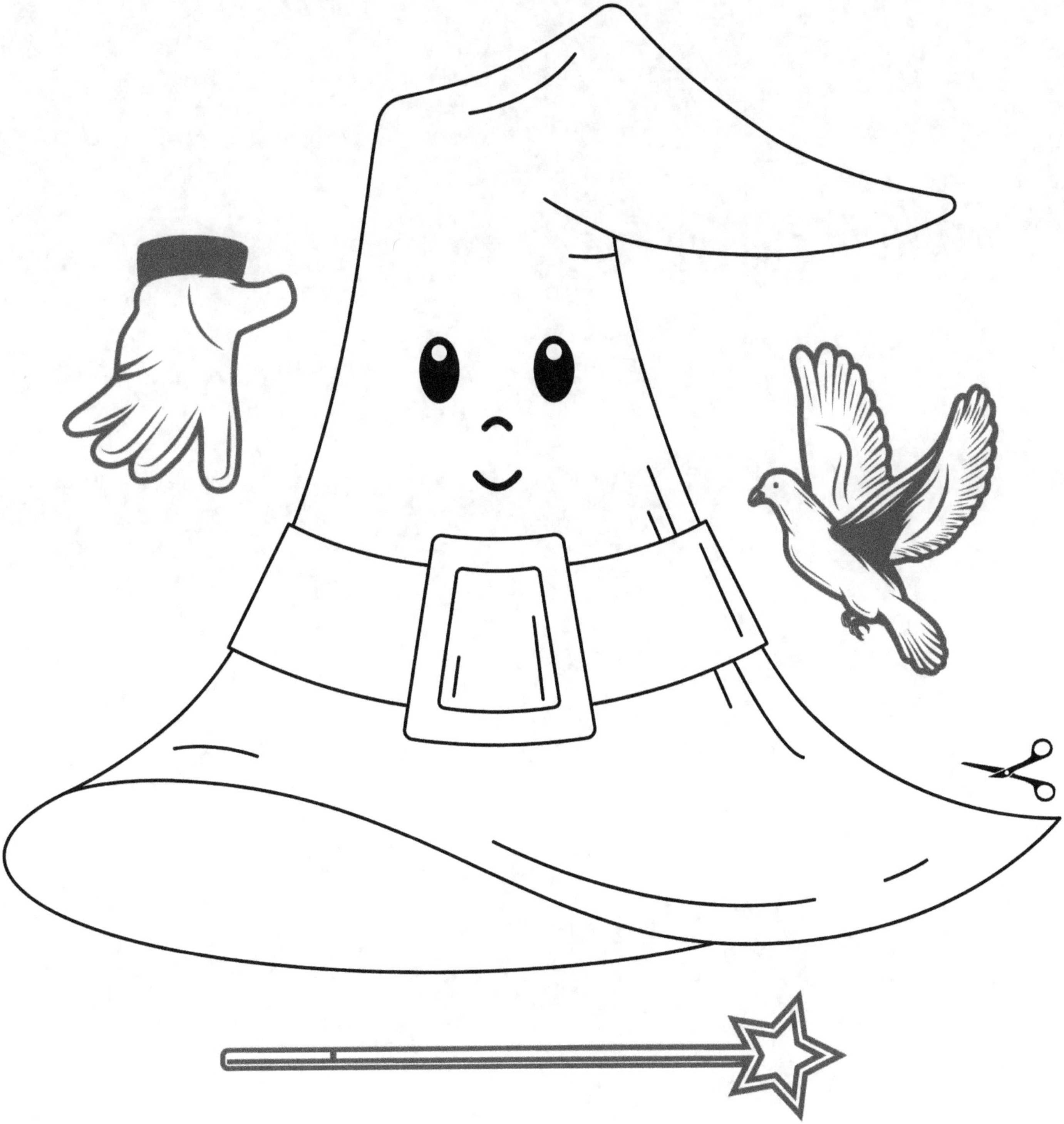

SHAMROCKS

Color the shamrocks and cut them out

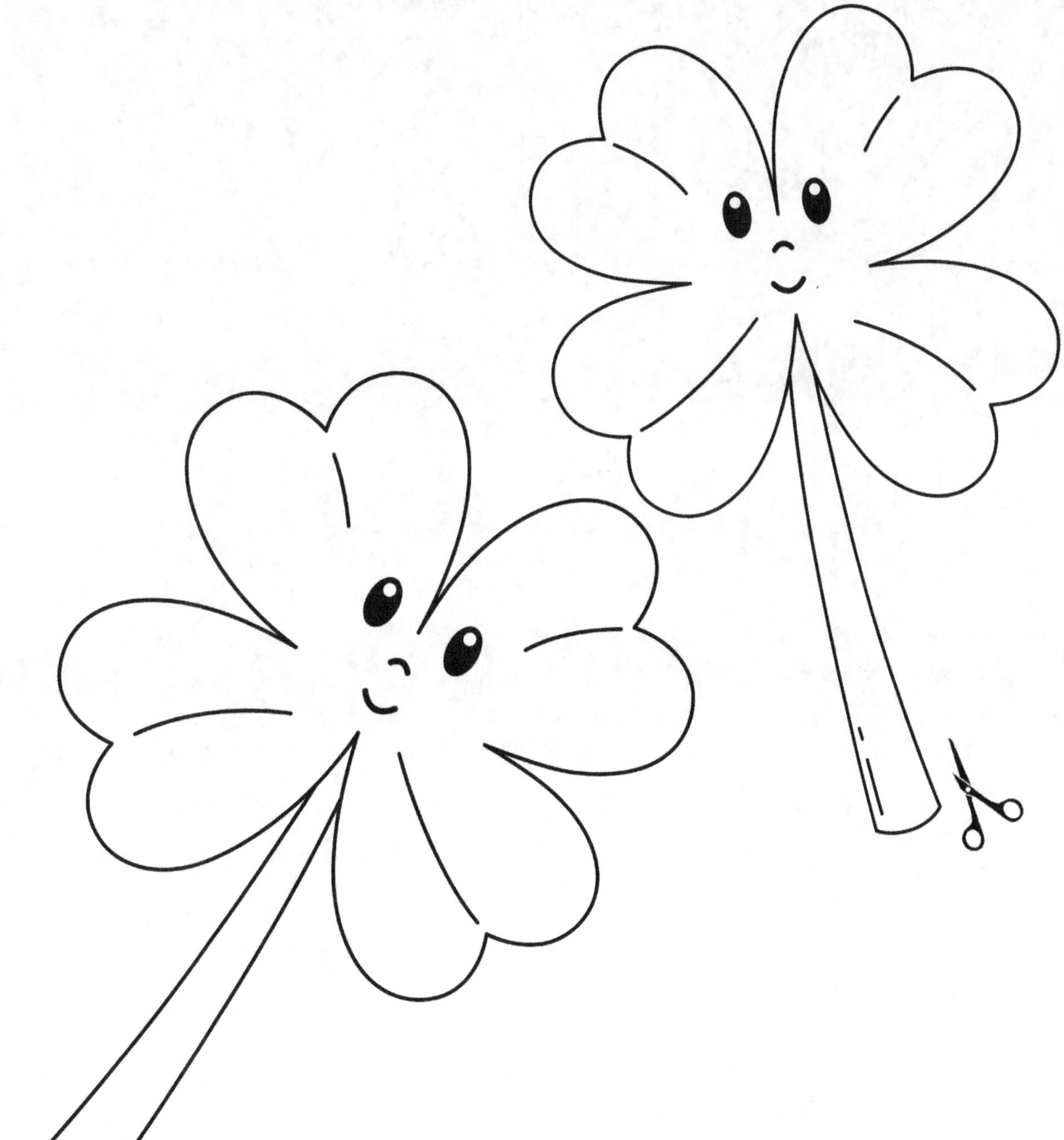

DINOSAUR

LEVEL

Color the dinosaur then cut it out

BELL

Color and cut out the bell

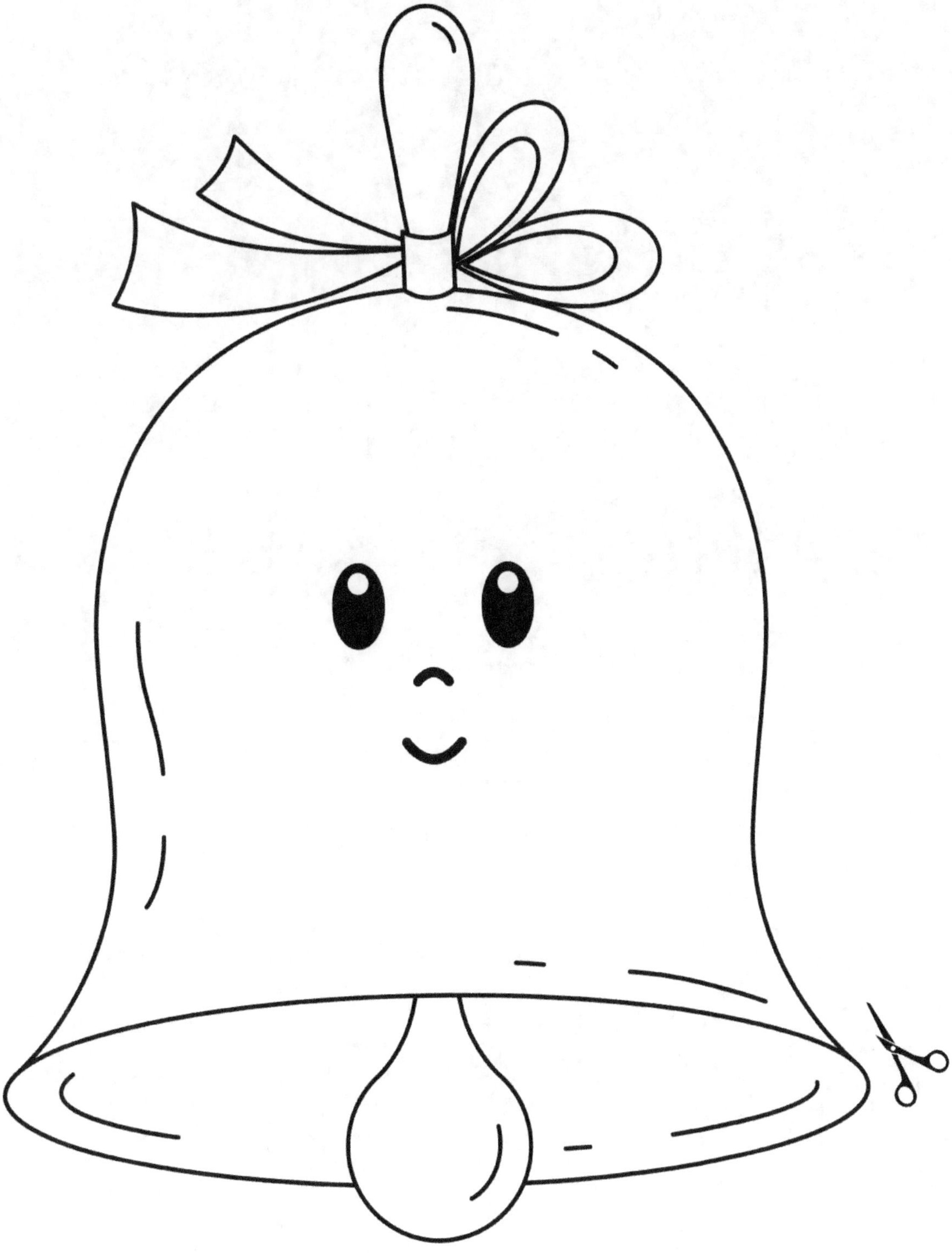

BUTTERFLY

Color each of the butterflies and then cut out the bottom one

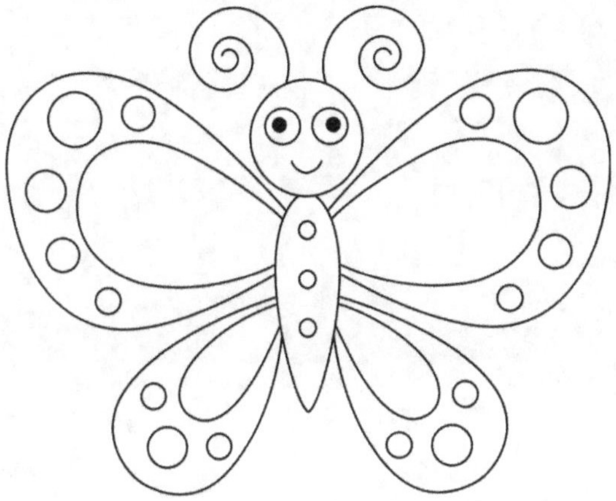

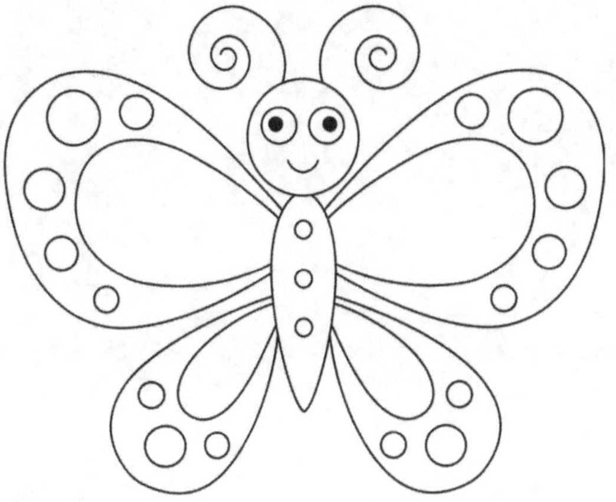

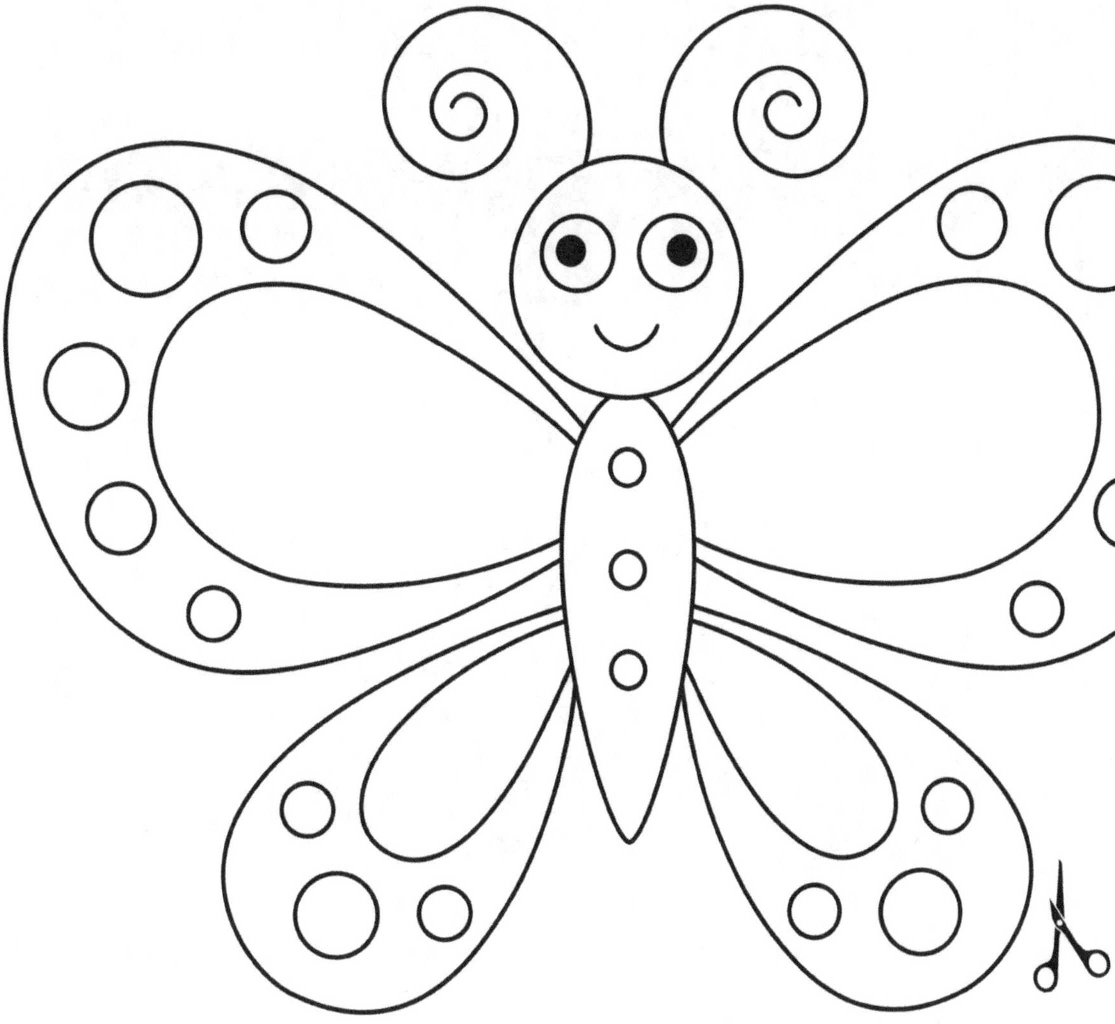

CUPCAKE

Color the cupcake and then cut it out

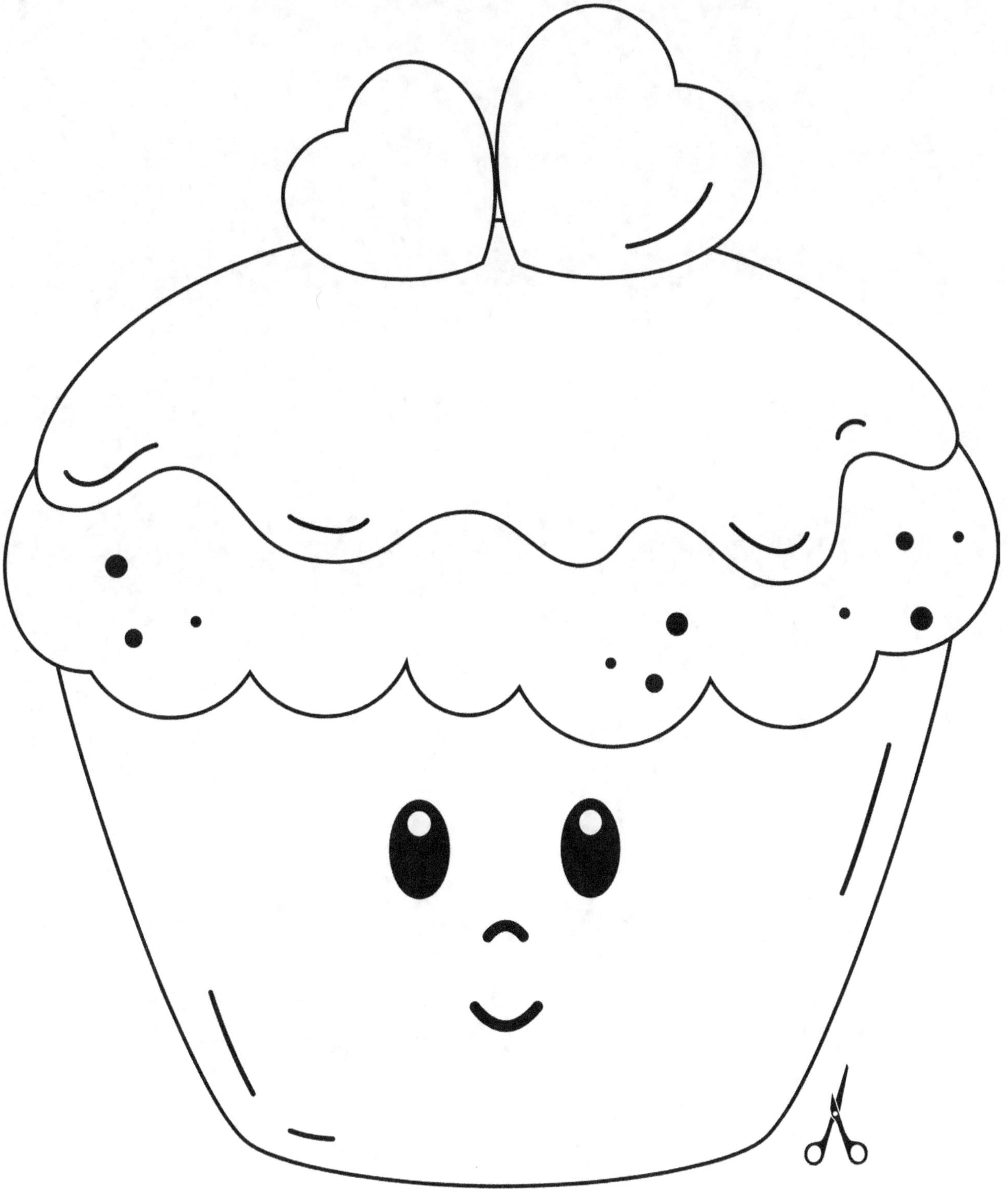

BEAR

Color the bear and then cut it out

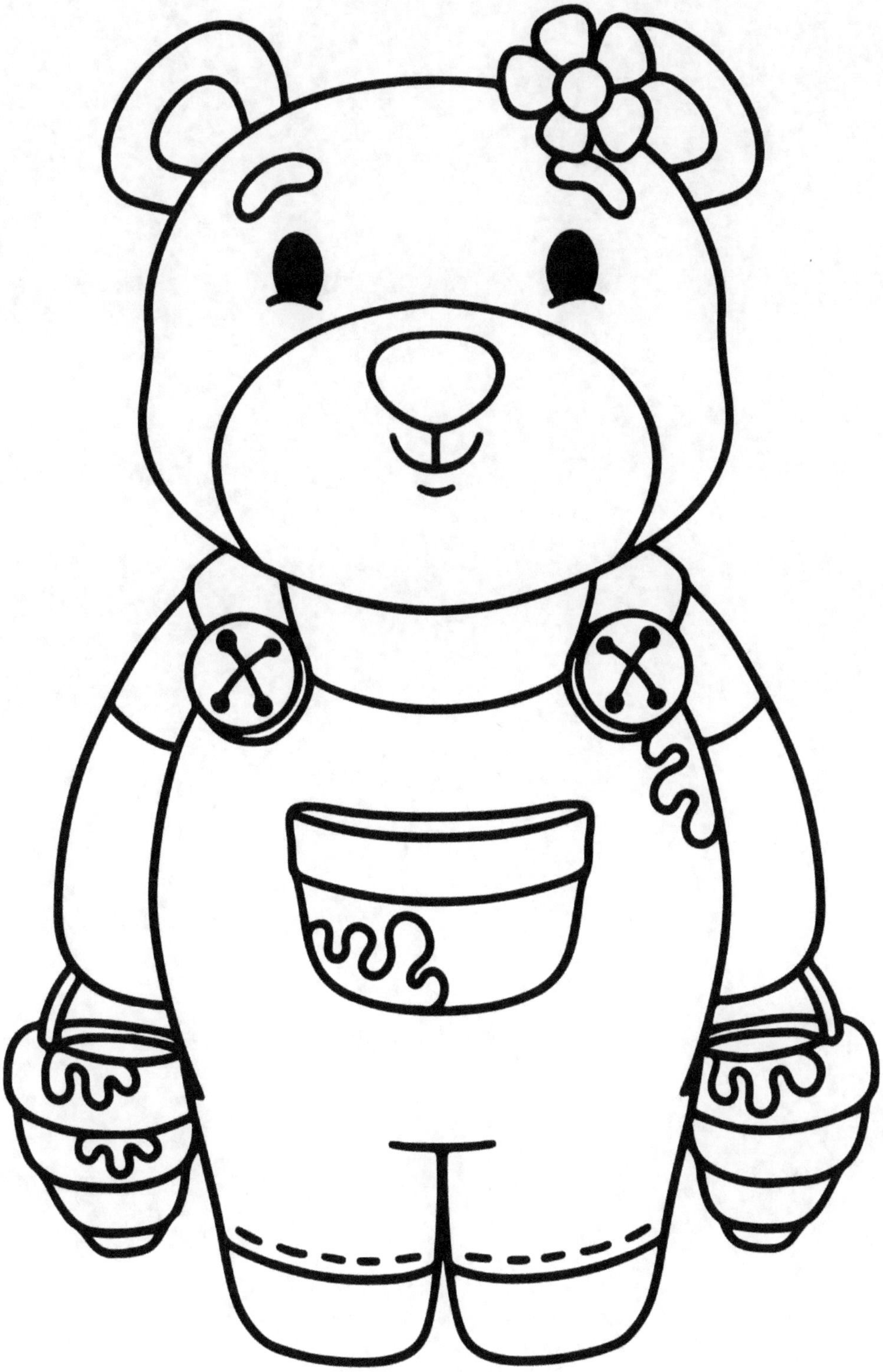

PUPPY

Color the puppy and then cut it out

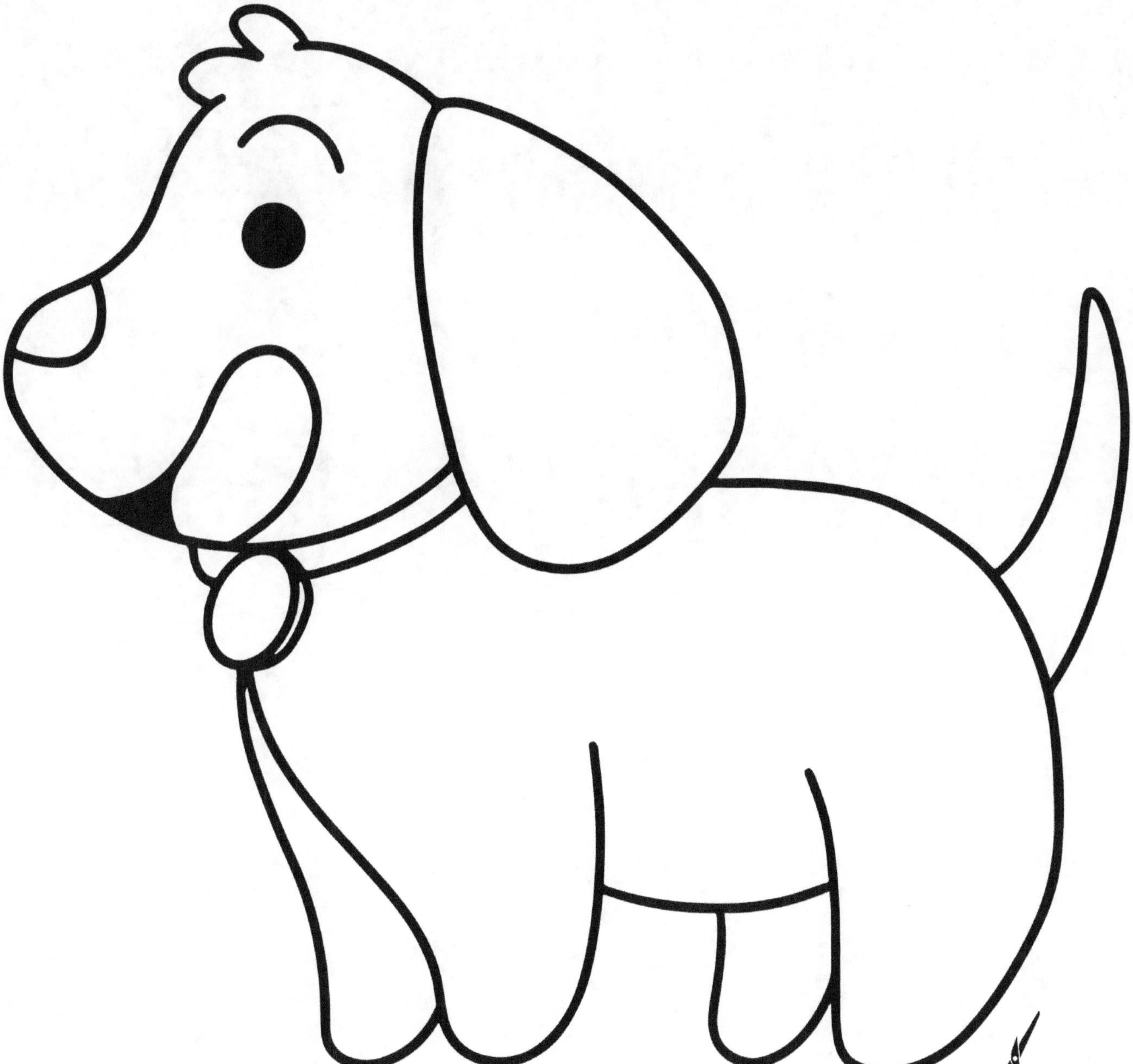

SPIDER

Color and cut out the spider

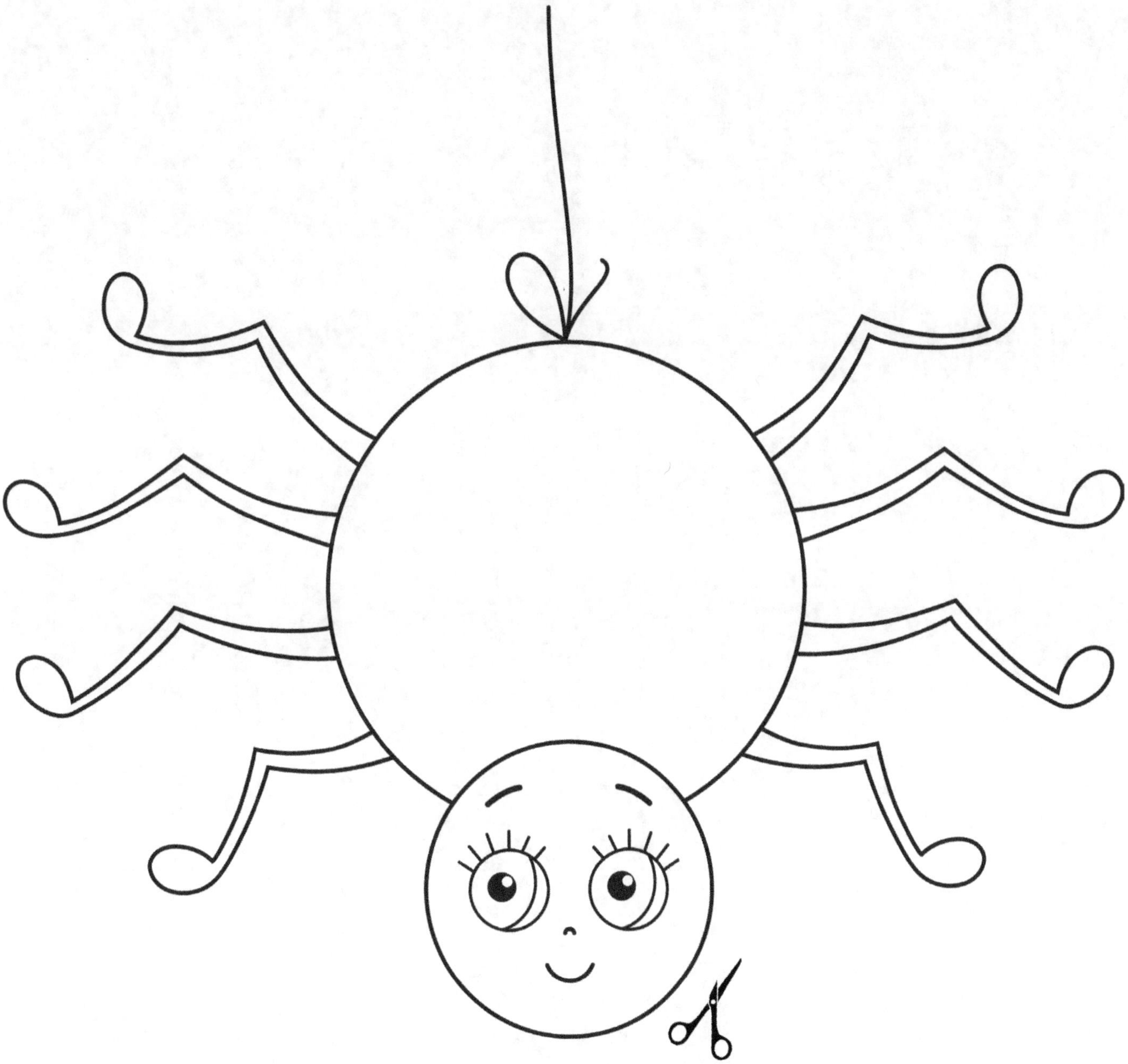

CUT & MATCH

Color each image, cut out, and match the other half

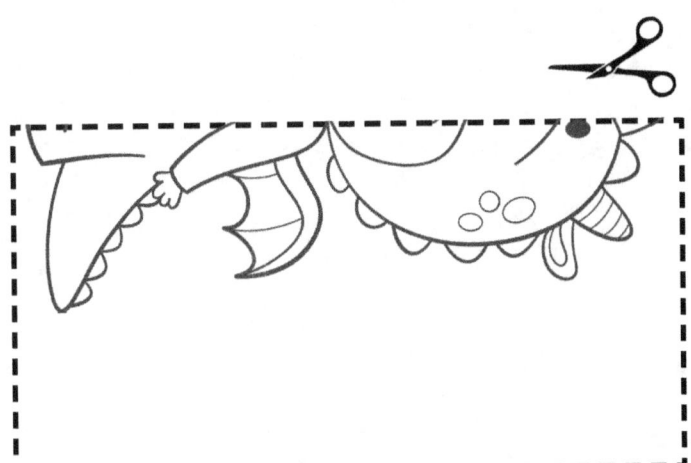

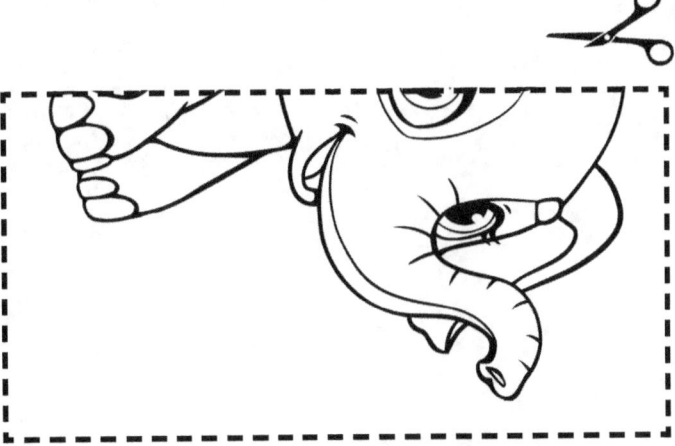

CUT & MATCH

Color each image, cut out, and match the other half

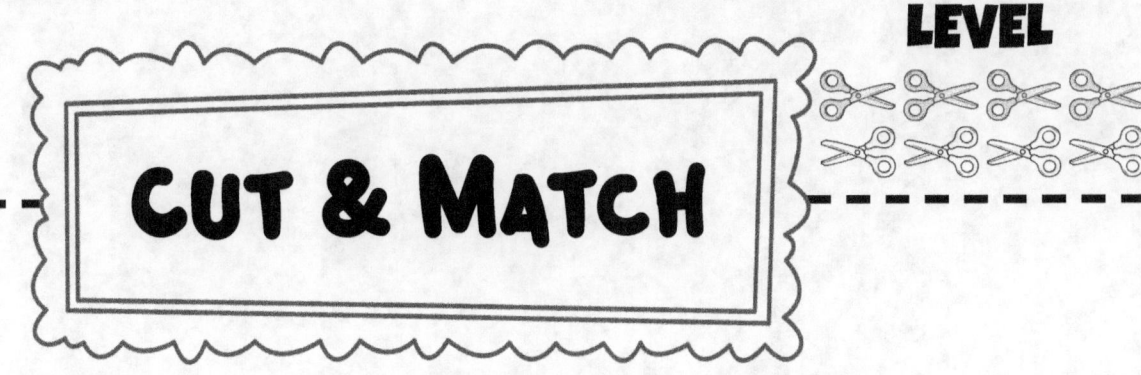

CUT & MATCH

LEVEL

Color each image, cut out, and match the other half

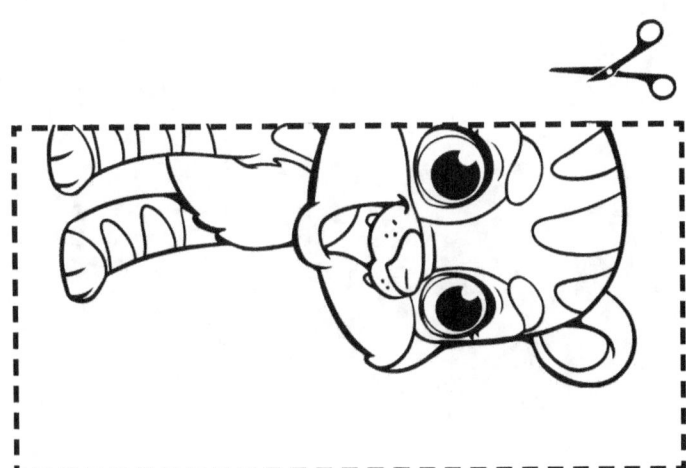

CUT & MATCH

Color each image, cut out, and match the other half

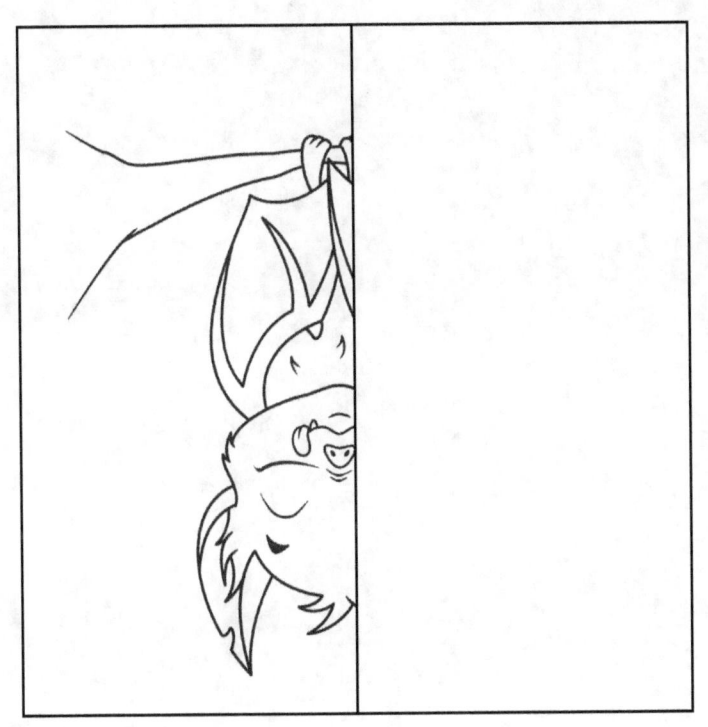

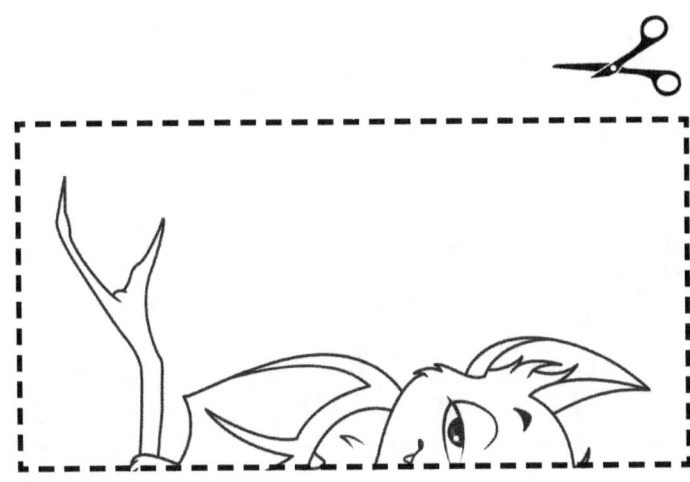

CUT & MATCH

LEVEL

Color each image, cut out, and match the other half

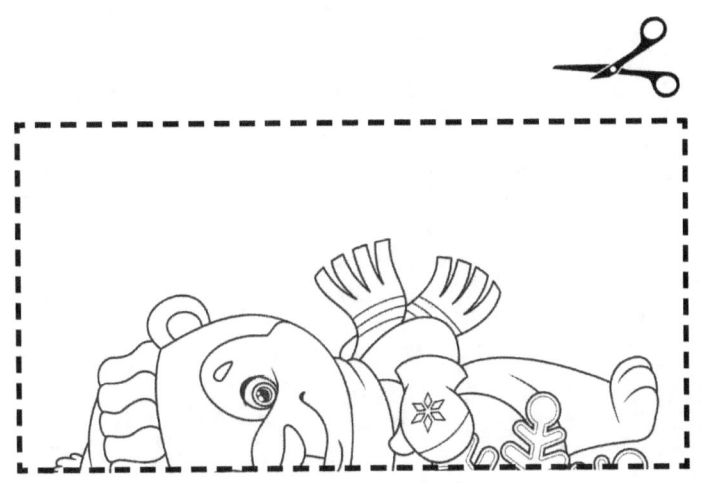

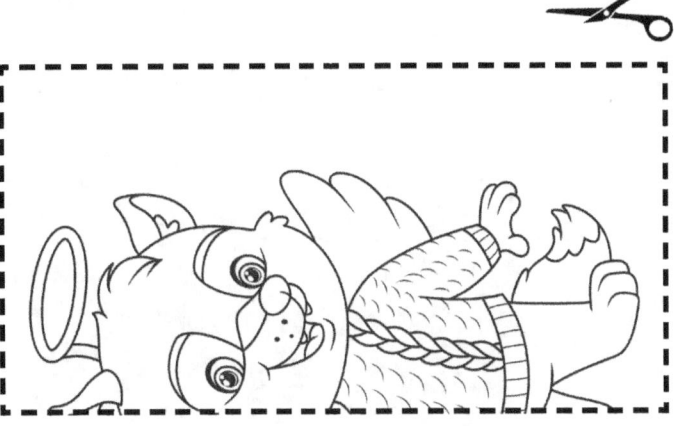

CUT & MATCH

Color each image, cut out, and match the other half

CUT & MATCH

Cut out each piece, match, and color the complete image

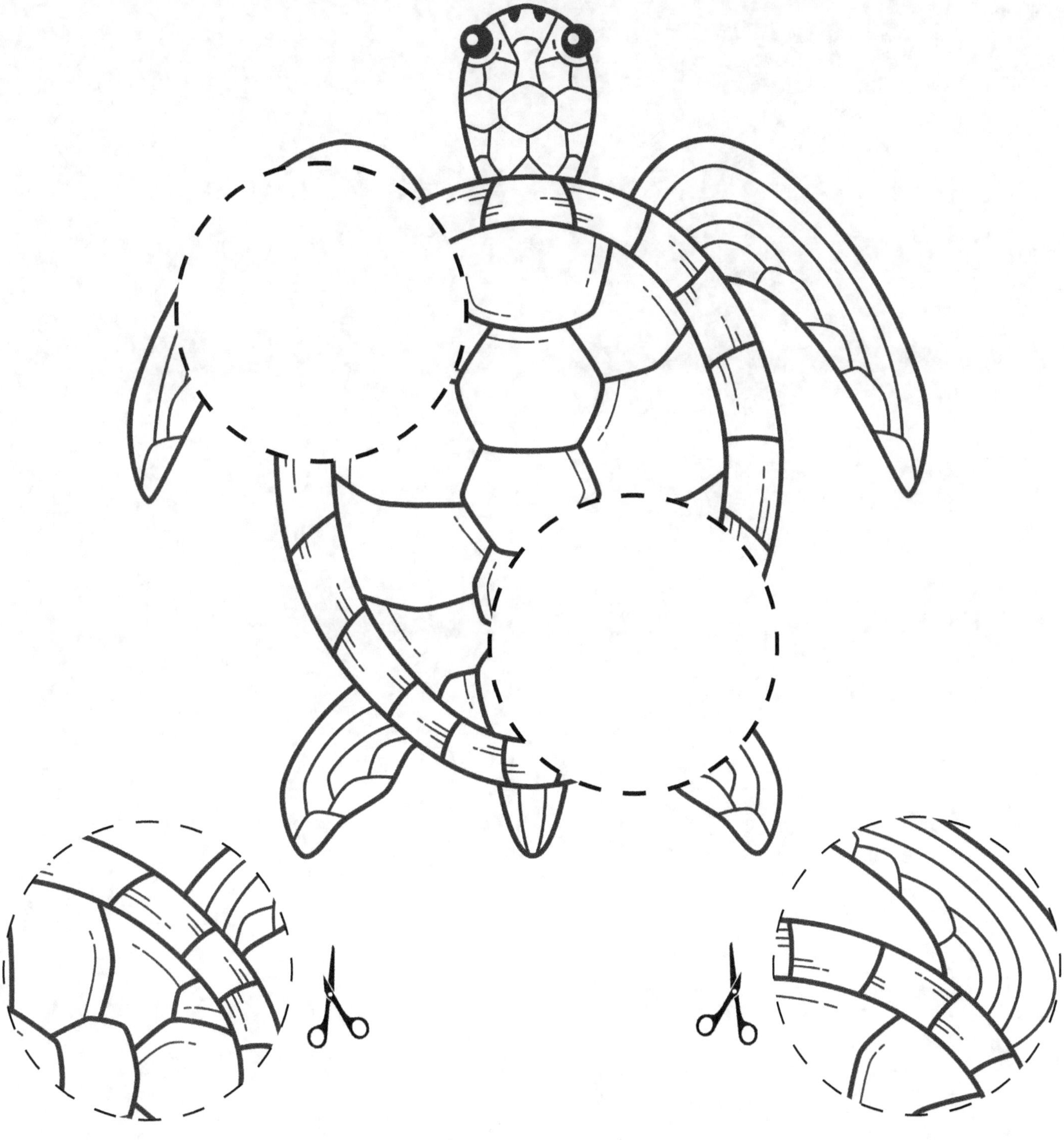

CUT & MATCH

Cut out each piece, match, and color the complete image

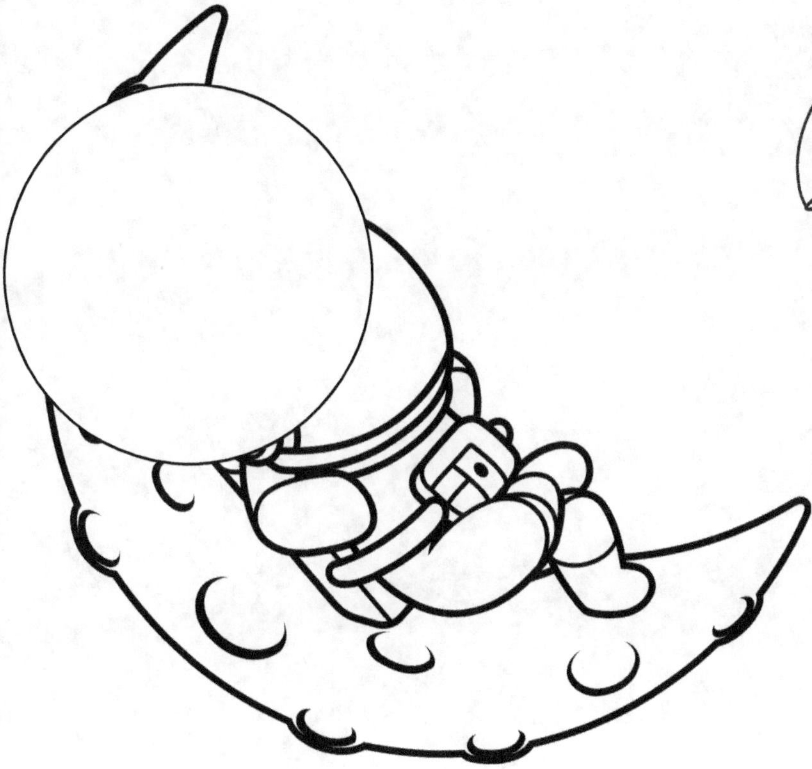

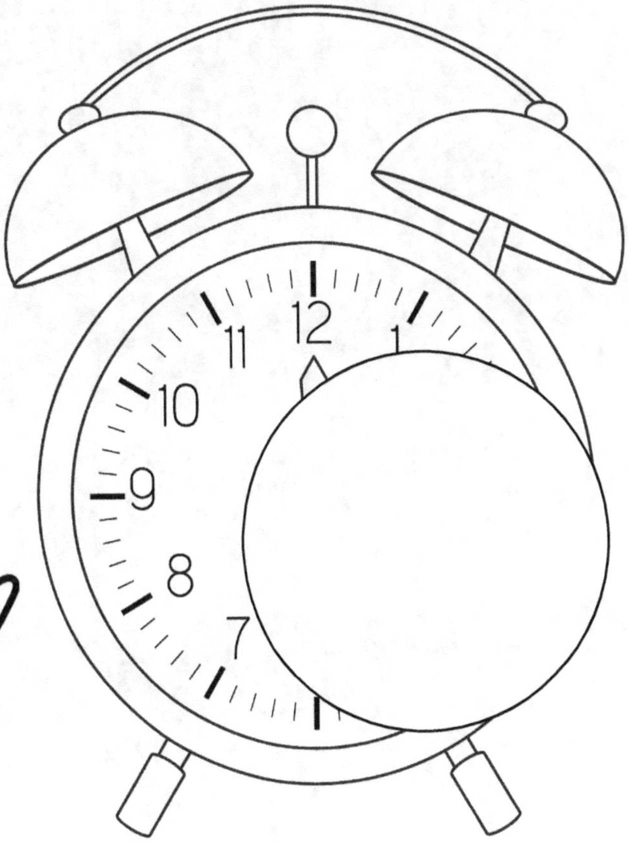

CUT & MATCH

Cut out each piece, match, and color the complete image

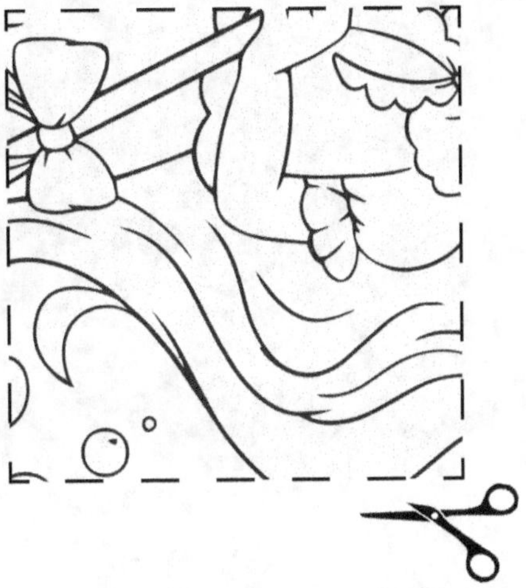

CUT & MATCH

Cut out each piece, match, and color the complete image

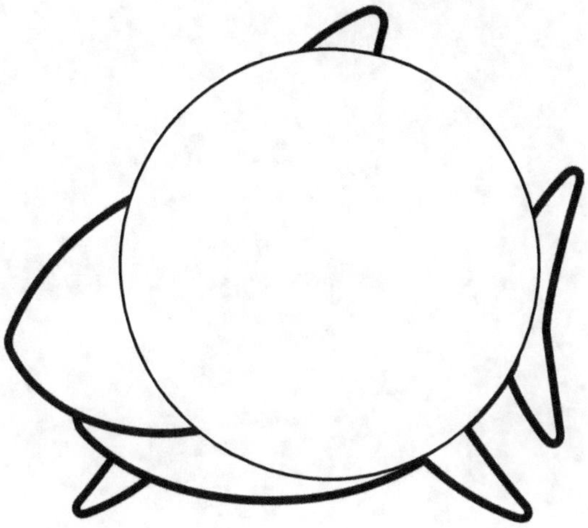

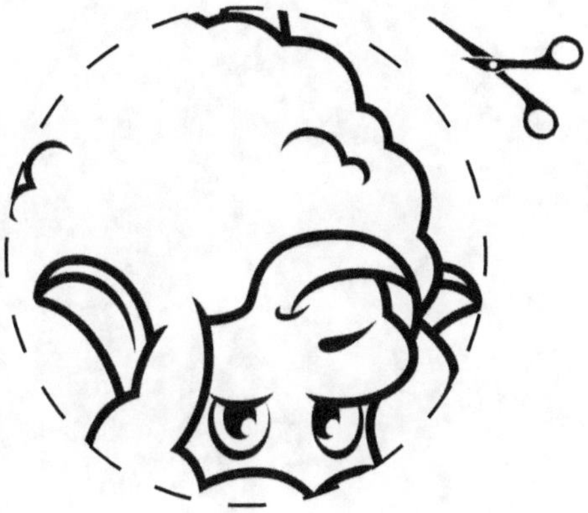

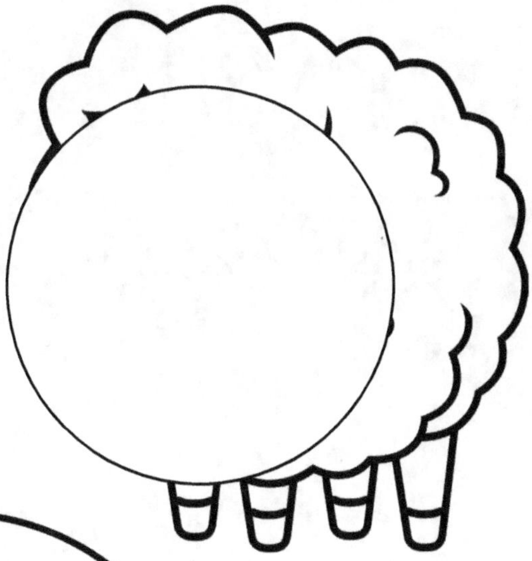

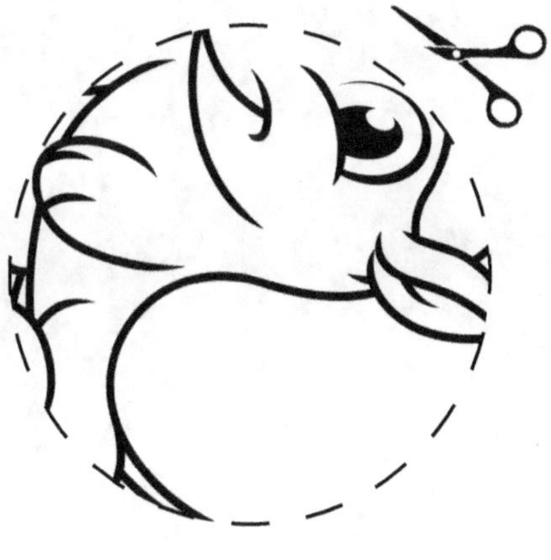

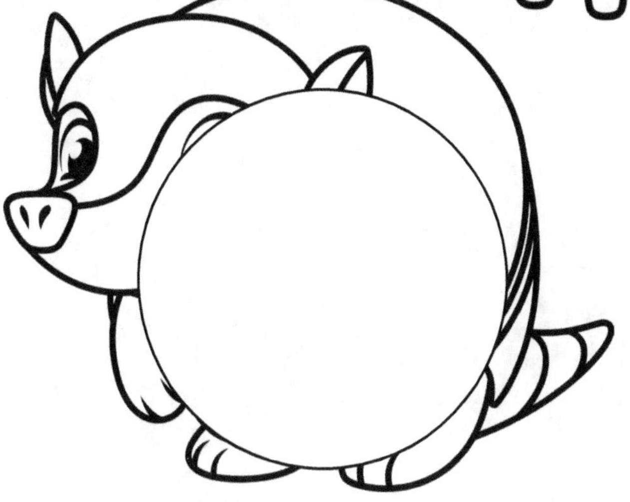

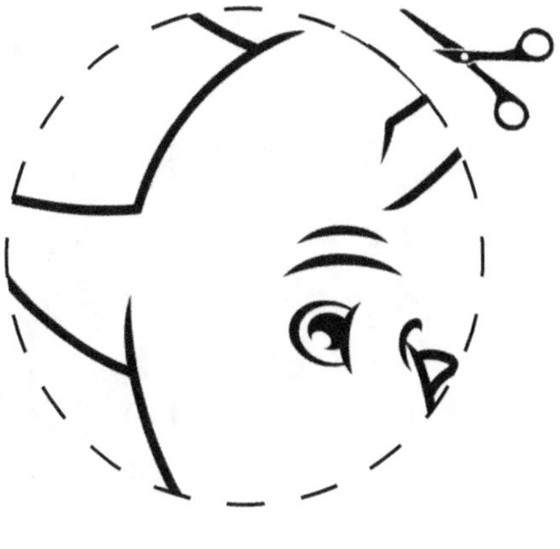

CUT & MATCH

Cut out each piece, match, and color the complete image

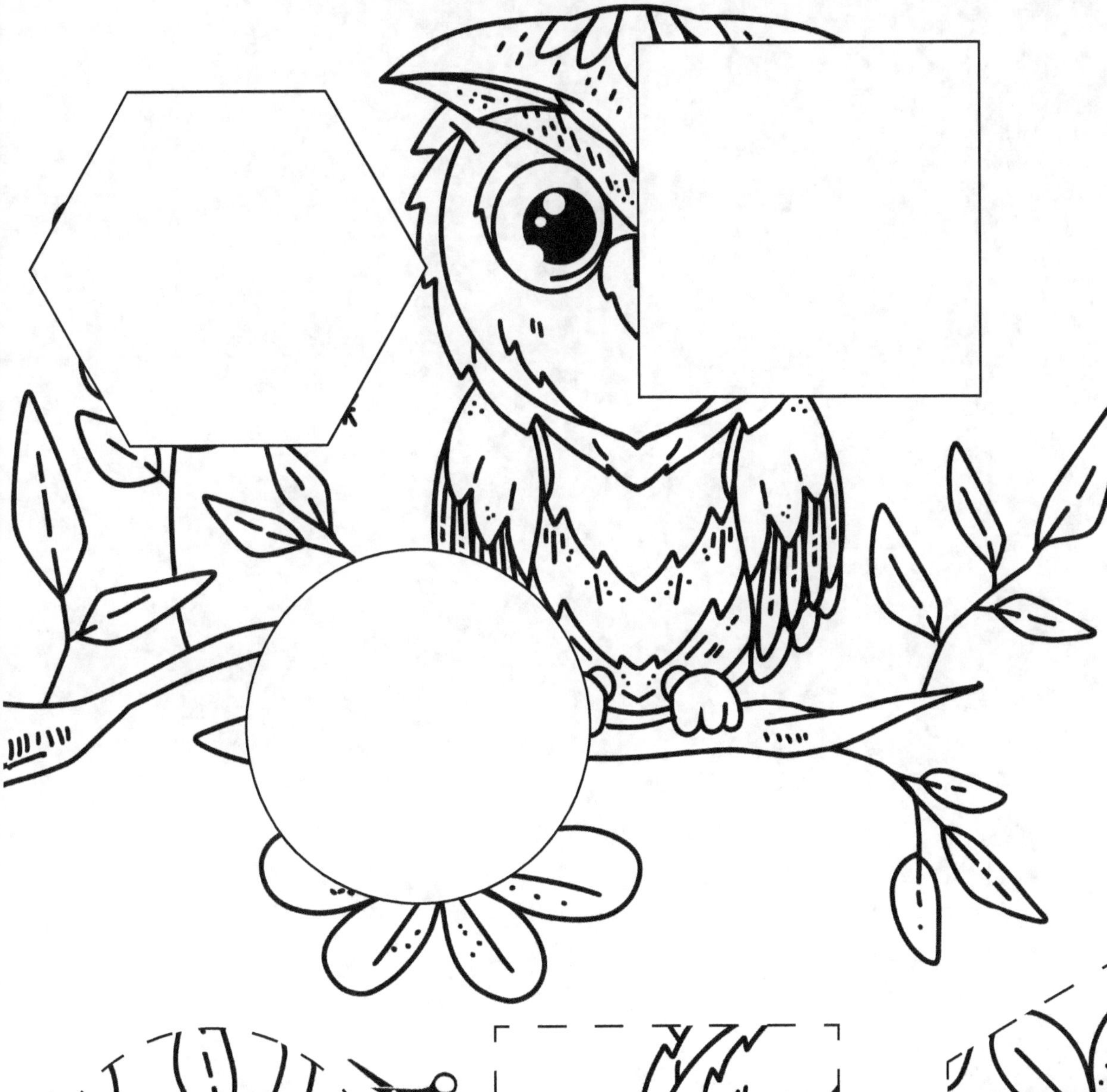

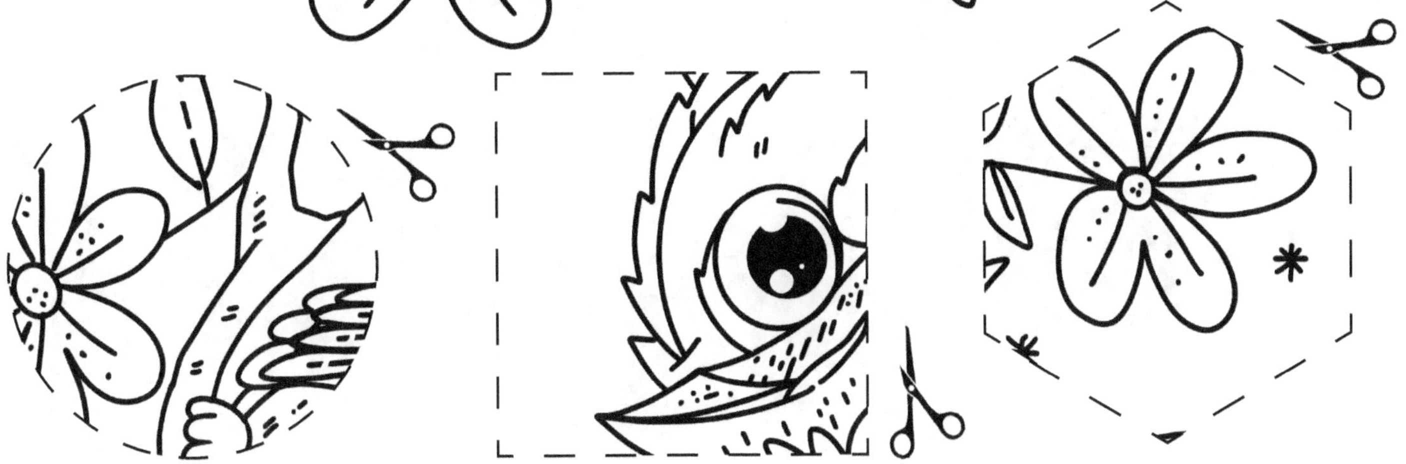

CUT & MATCH

Cut out each piece, match, and color the complete image

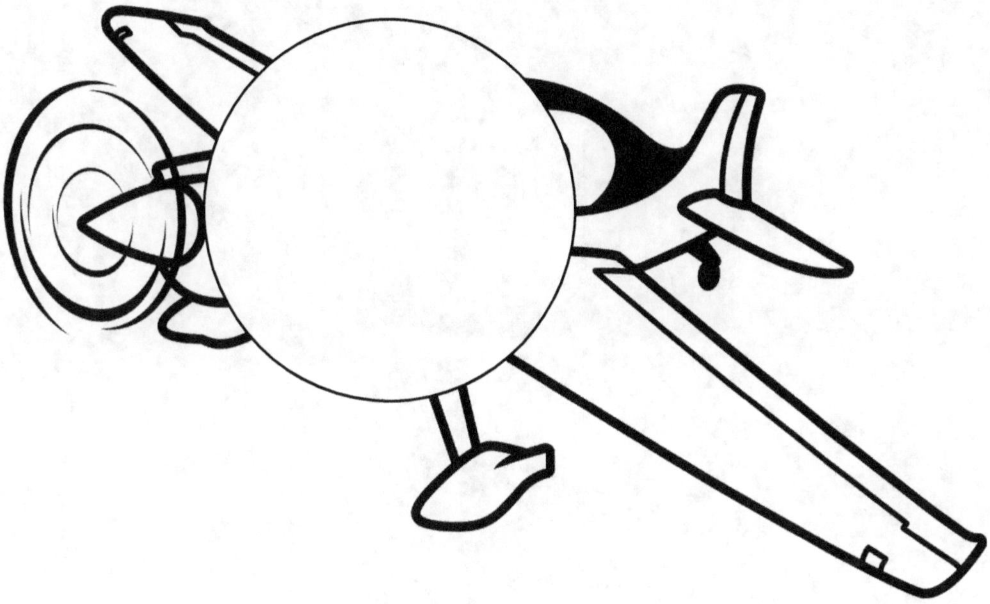

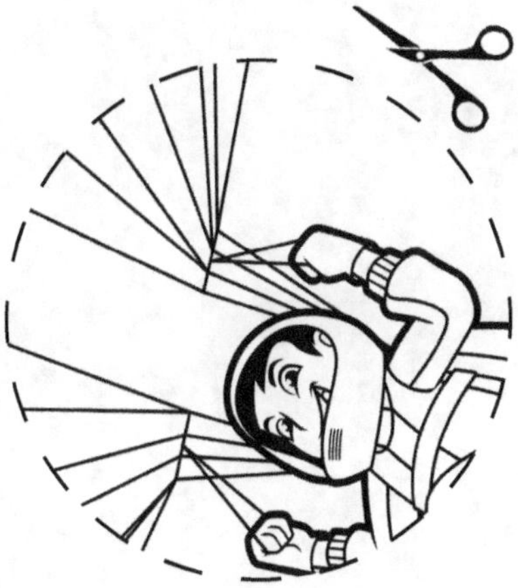

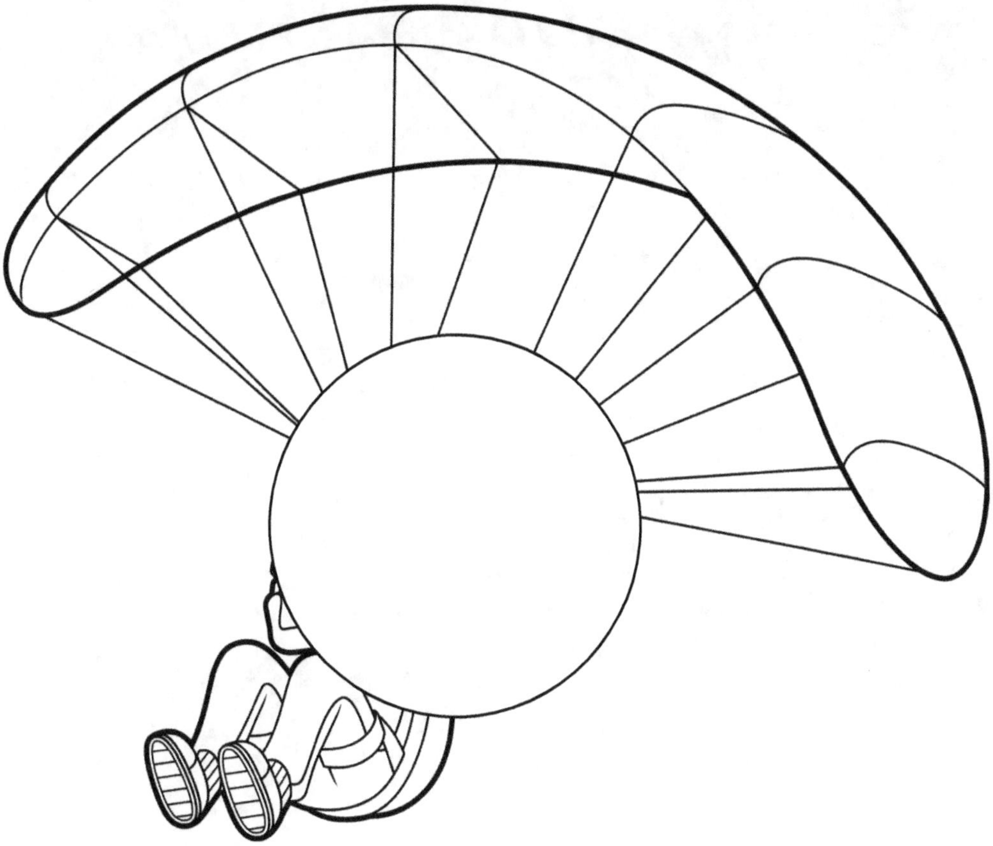

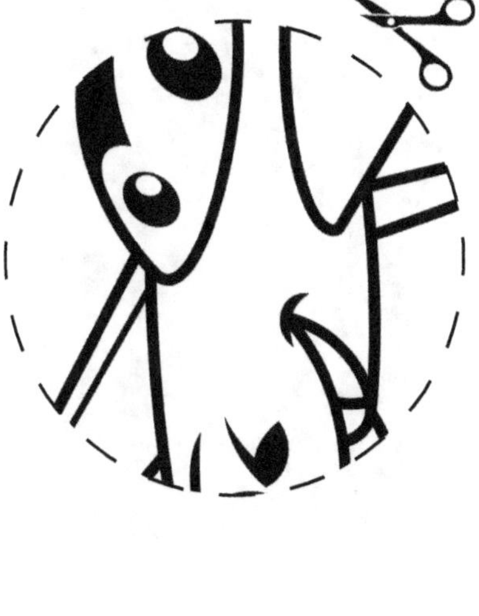

CUT & MATCH

Cut out each piece, match, and color the complete image

CUT & MATCH

Cut out each piece, match, and color the complete image

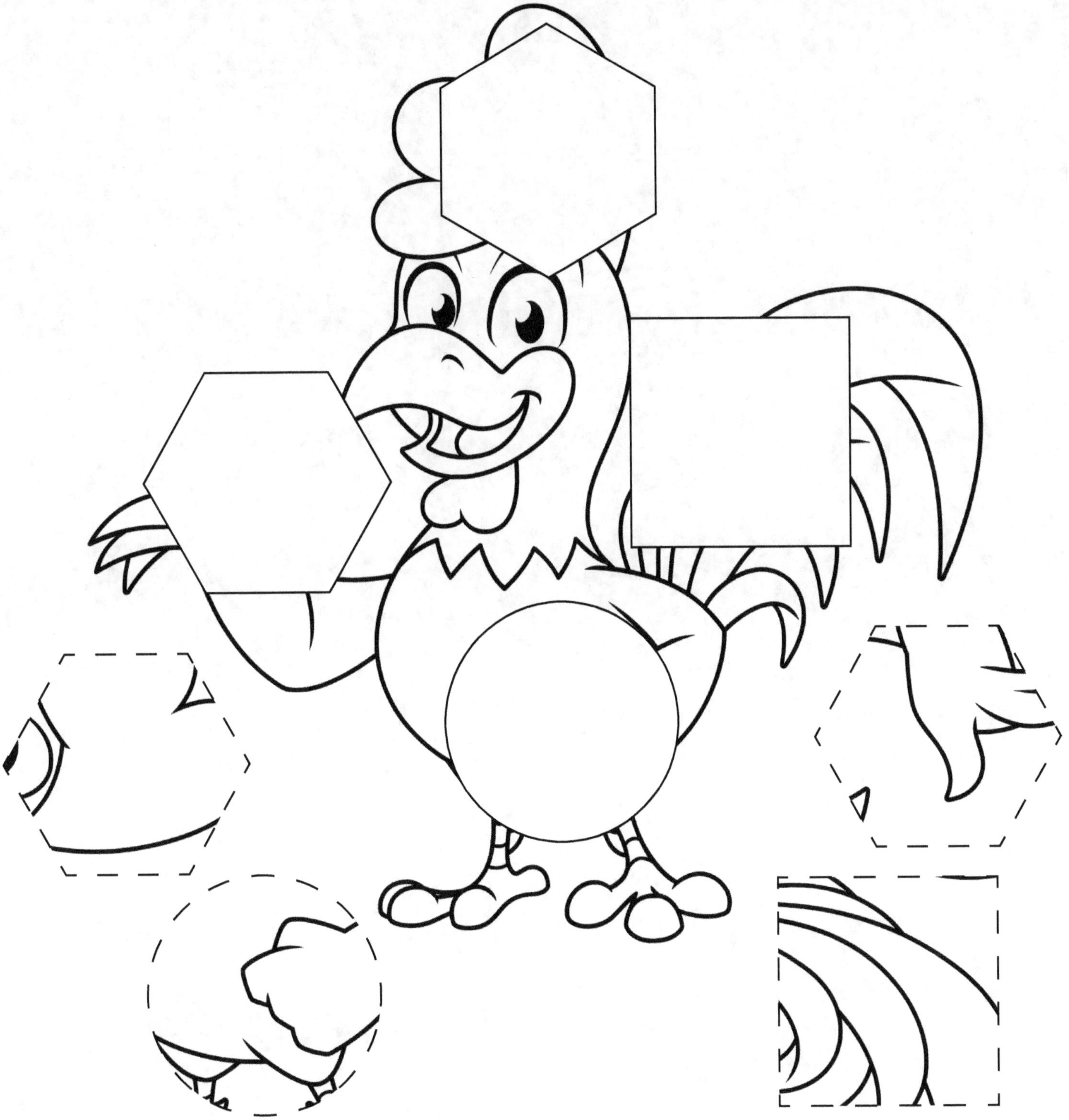

CUT & MATCH

LEVEL

Cut out each piece, match, and color the complete image

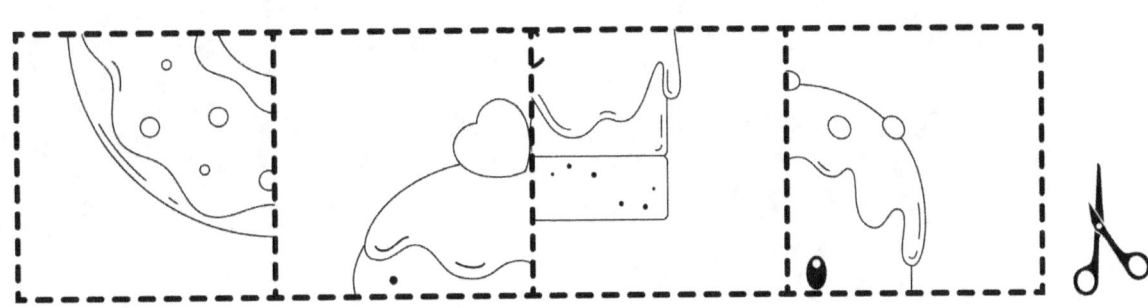

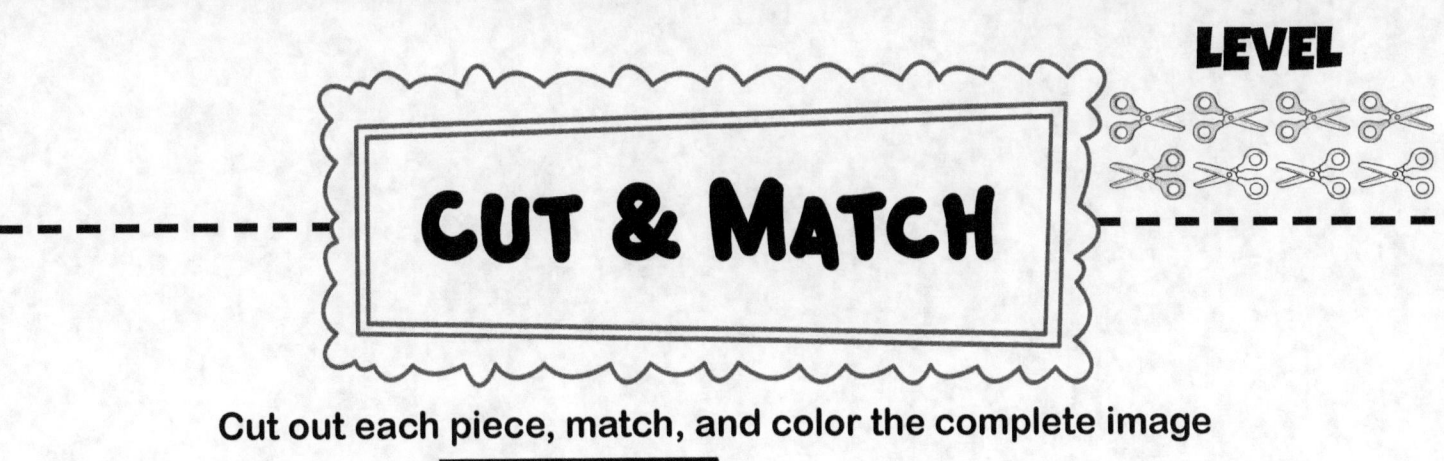
CUT & MATCH

Cut out each piece, match, and color the complete image

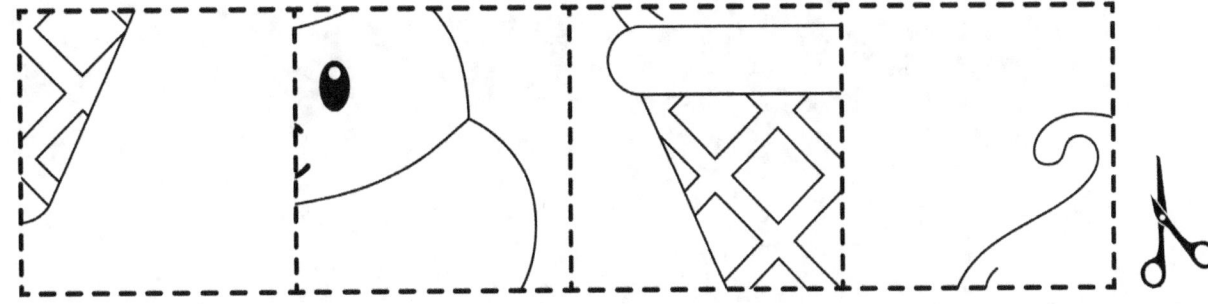

ARRANGE & PASTE

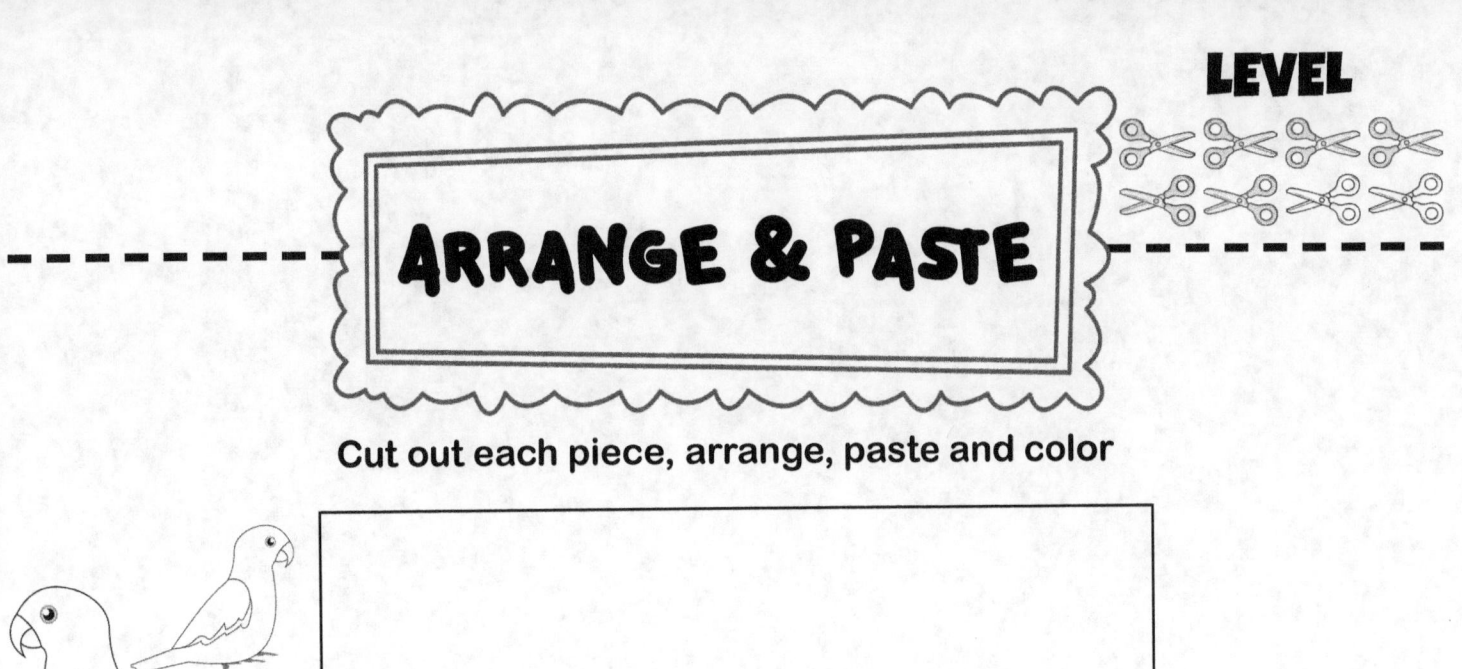

Cut out each piece, arrange, paste and color

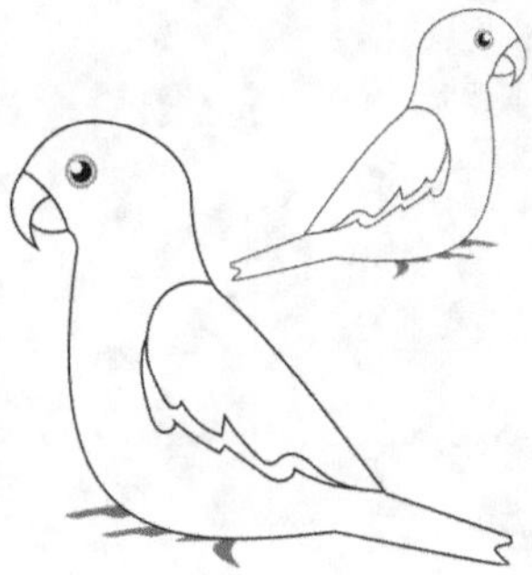

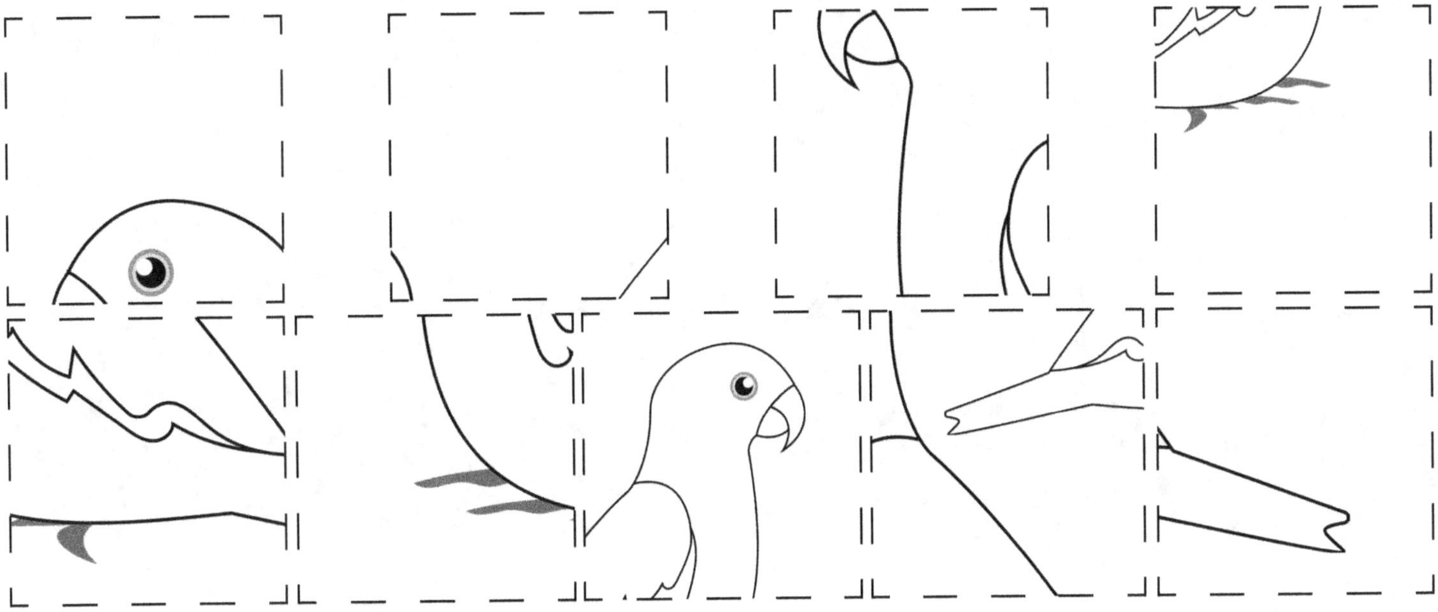

ARRANGE & PASTE

Cut out each piece, arrange, paste and color

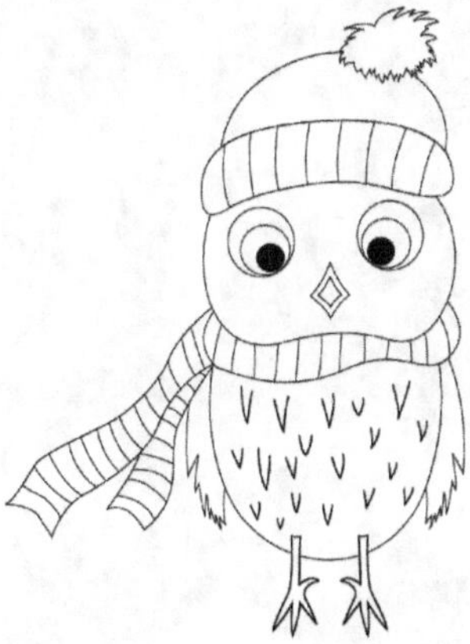

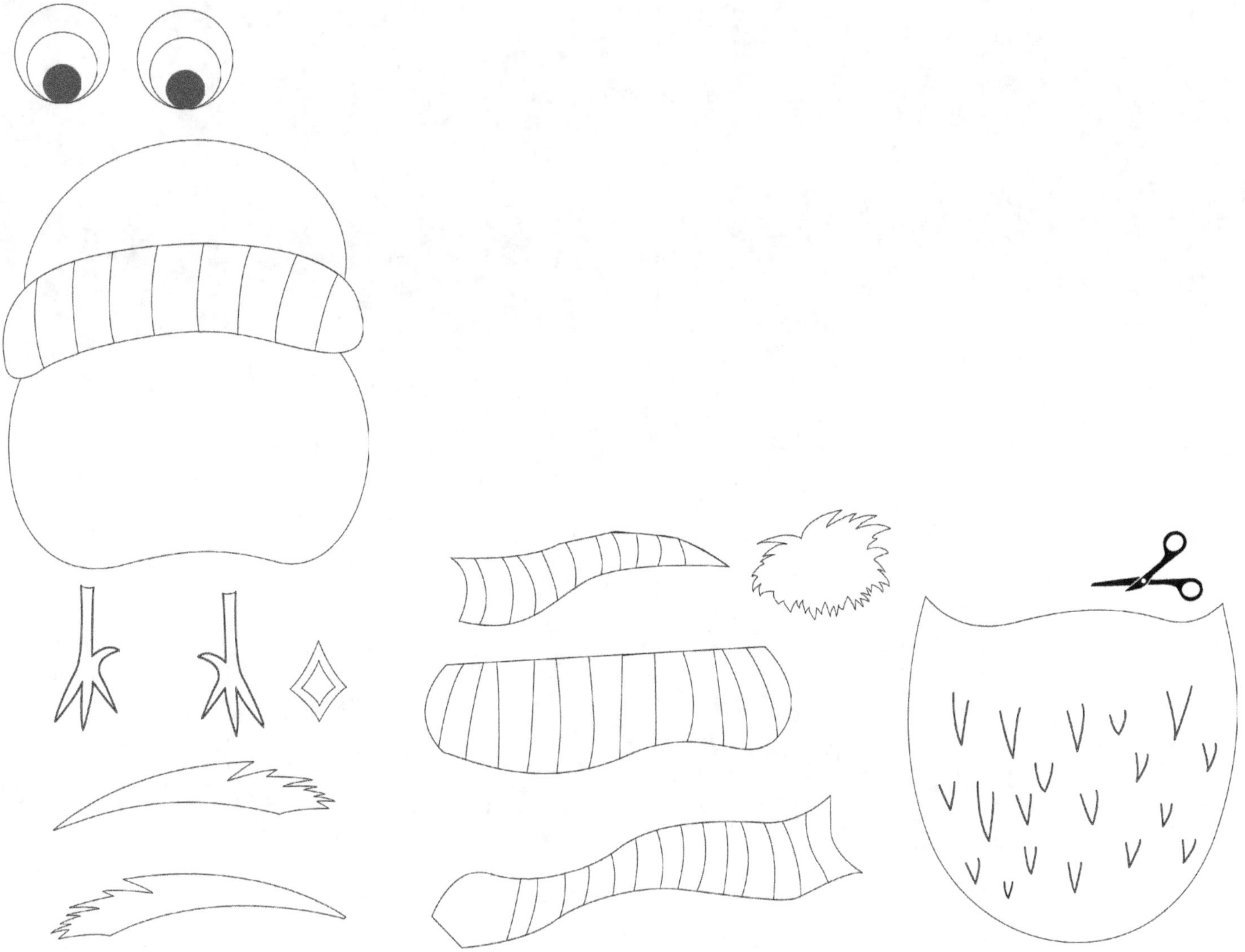

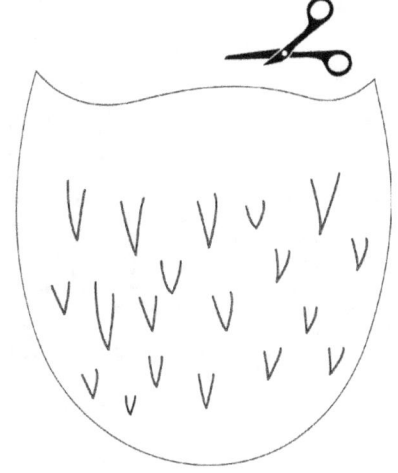

ARRANGE & PASTE

Cut out each piece, arrange, paste and color

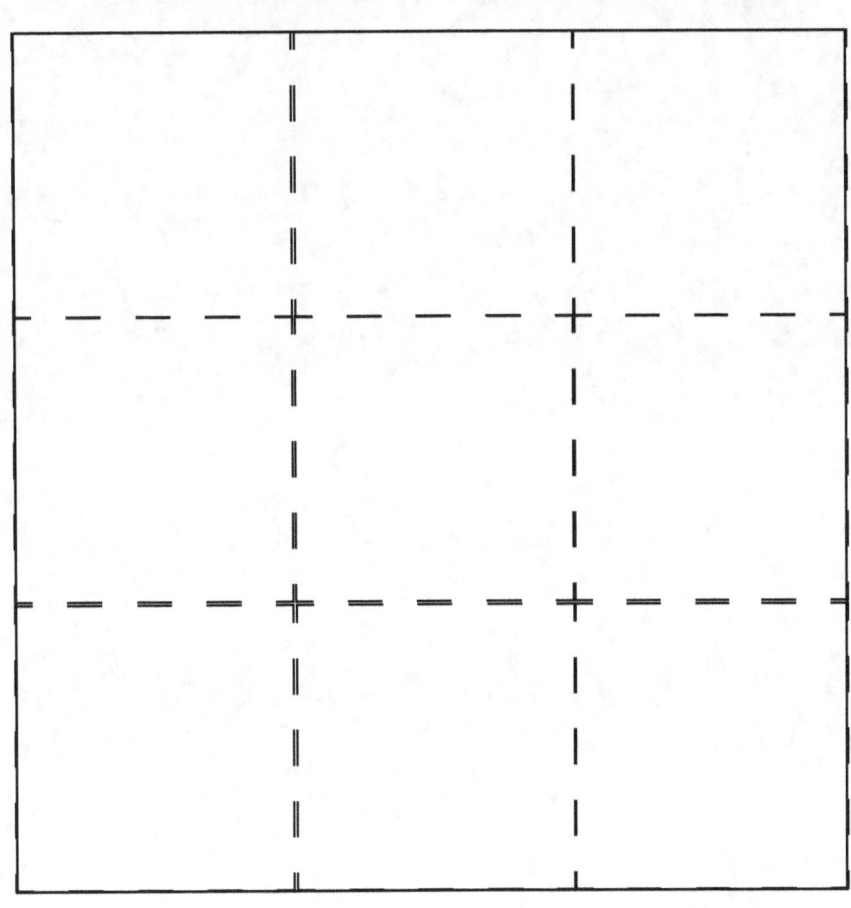

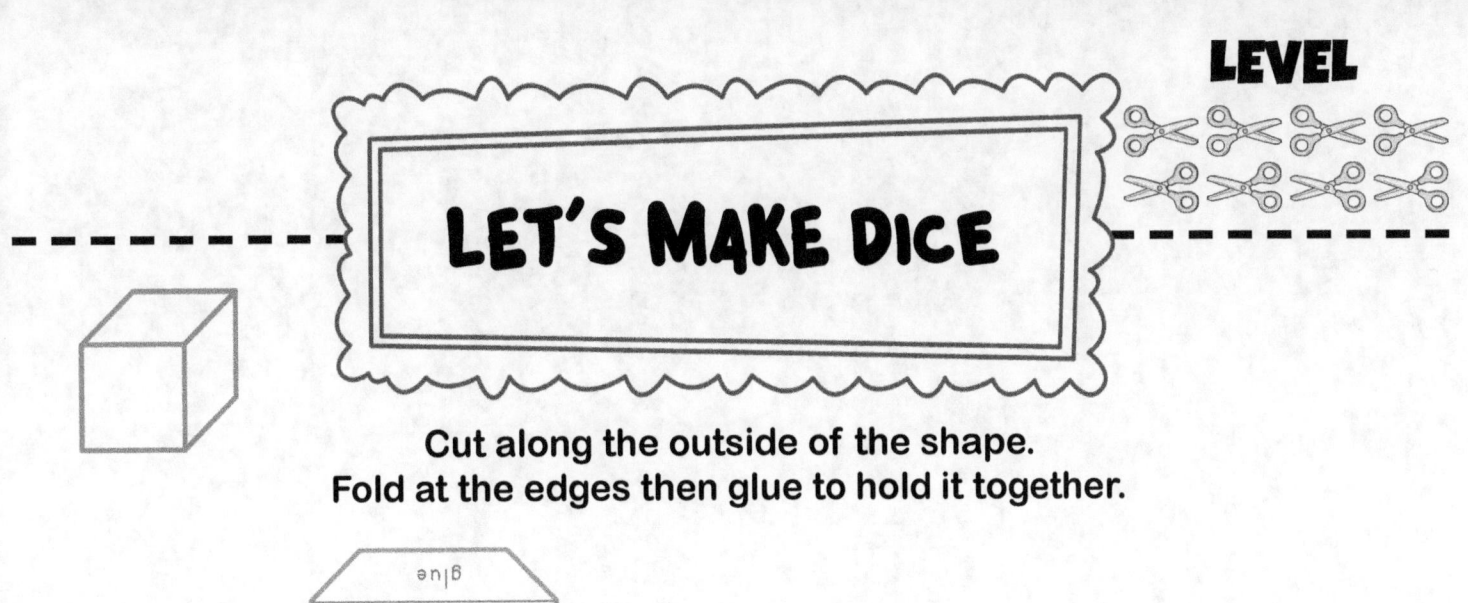

LET'S MAKE DICE

Cut along the outside of the shape.
Fold at the edges then glue to hold it together.

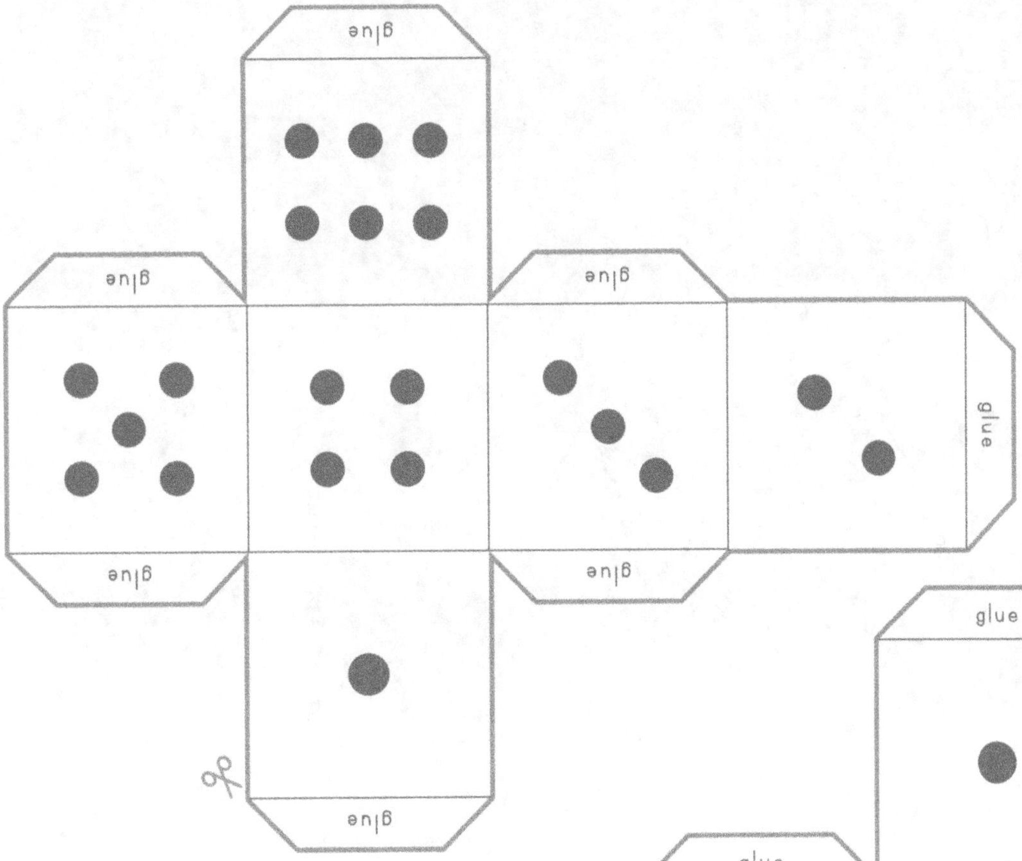

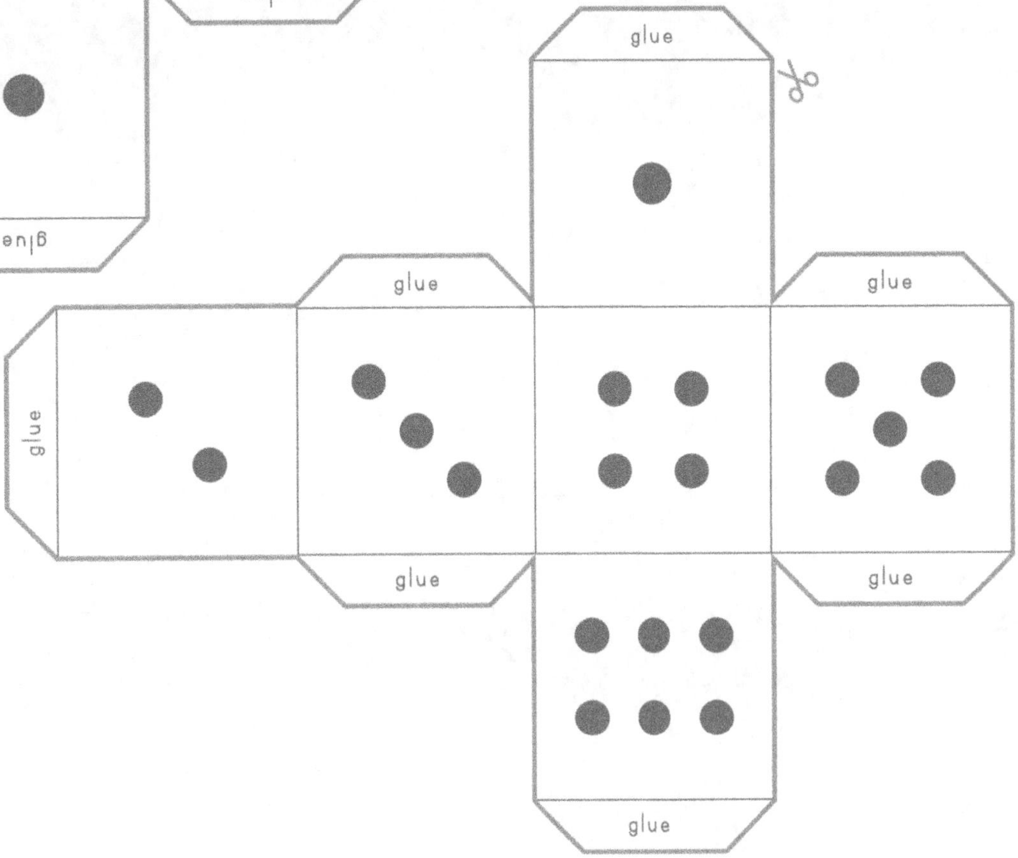

glue

glue

glue

glue

glue

glue

glue

glue

glue

glue

glue

glue

glue

glue

glue

glue

ARRANGE & PASTE

Cut out each piece, arrange, paste and color

ARRANGE & PASTE

LEVEL

Cut out each piece, arrange, paste and color

PEACOCK

Color the peacock then carefully cut it out

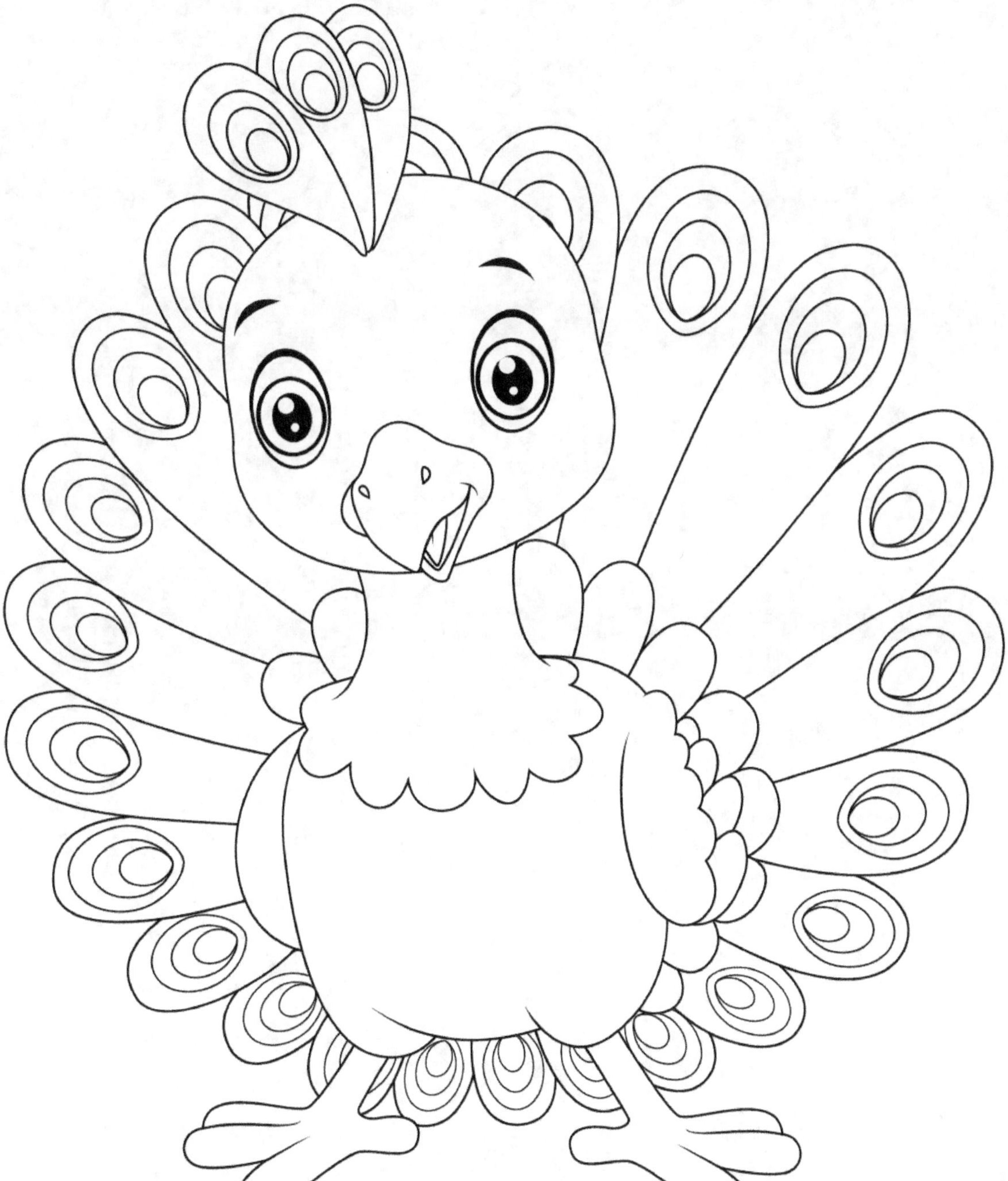

ARRANGE & PASTE

Cut out each piece, arrange, paste and color

ARRANGE & PASTE PART 1

Cut out each piece, arrange, and paste on the next page then color

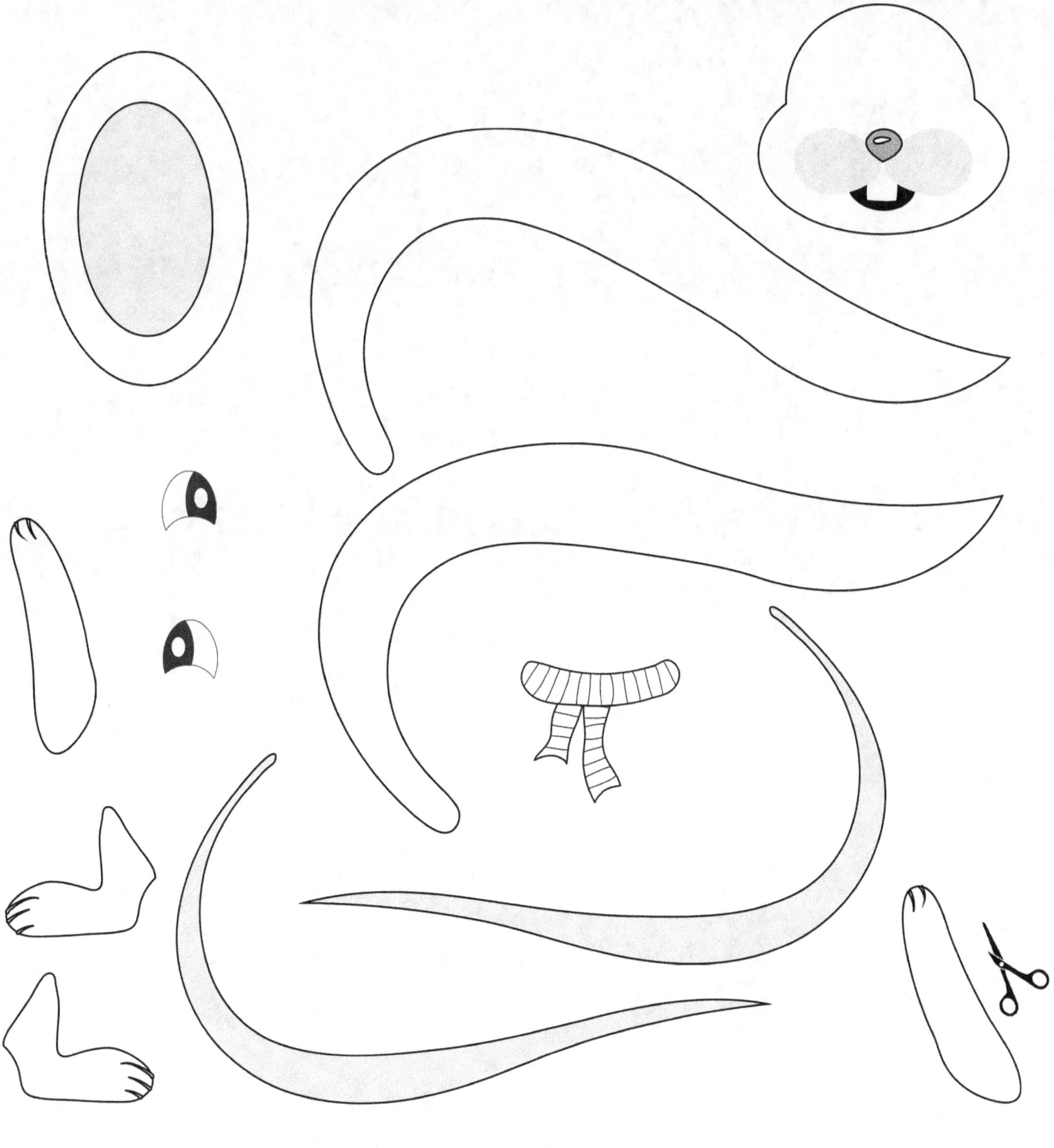

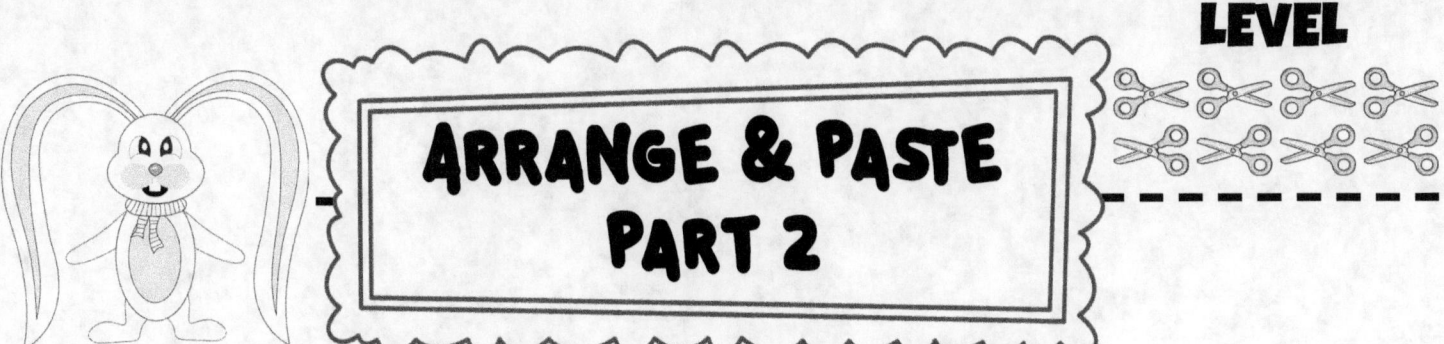

ARRANGE & PASTE PART 2

LEVEL

Arrange and paste the pieces from the previous page to make
the image on the left then color

OWL

Color the owl then carefully cut it out

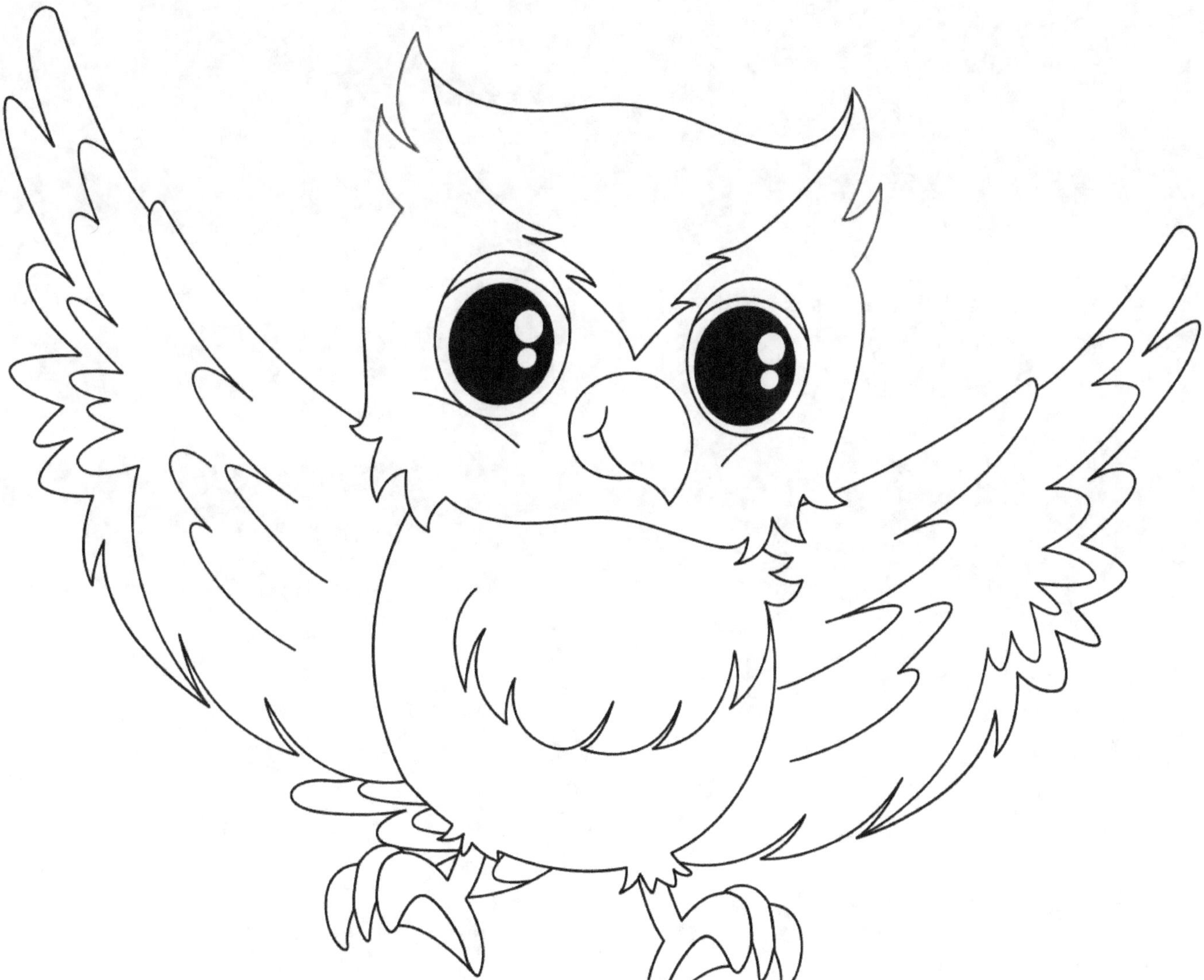

BEE

Color the bee then carefully cut it out

LEVEL

PENGUIN

Color the penguin then carefully cut it out

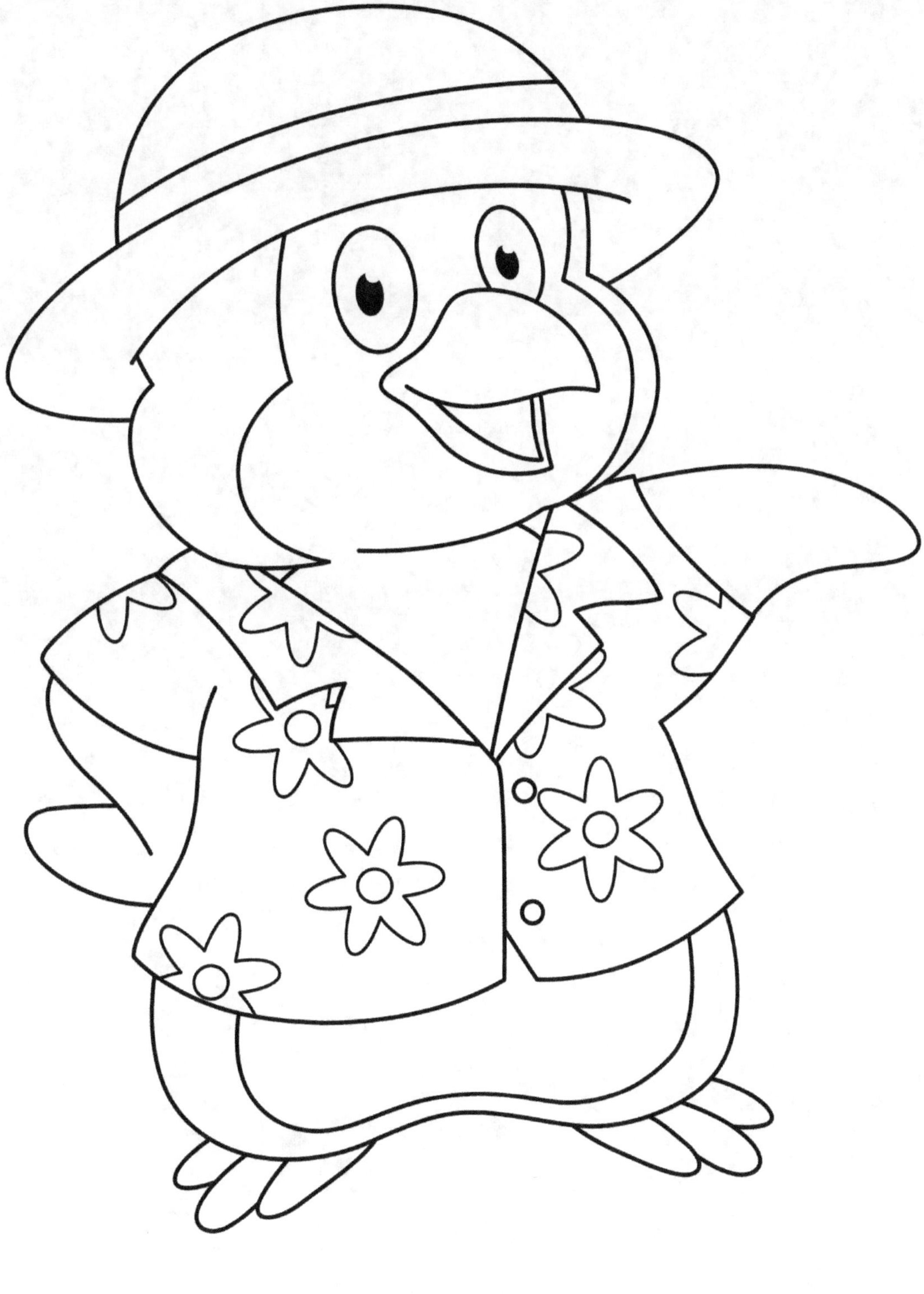

PIRATE

Color the pirate then carefully cut him out

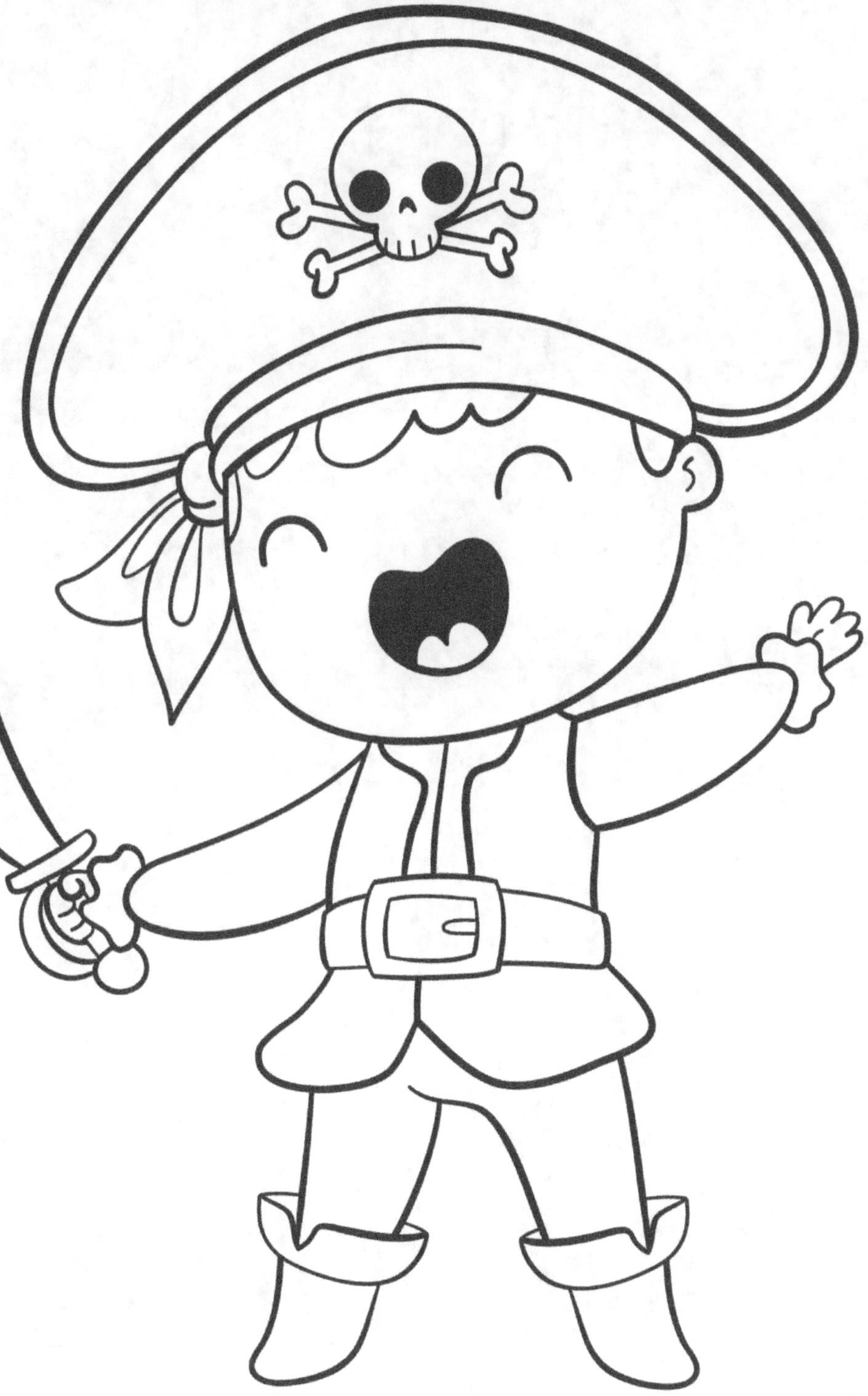

Free Coloring Book for Kids!

This fun printable coloring book is a blast and keeps

kids engaged for hours!

It's filled with cute doodles, animals, and so much more!

Get Your Copy Here:

https://bit.ly/3dfULw0